NAIC Investing for Life
Youth Handbook

Written by Fritz Williams
for the National Association of Investors Corporation

Published by National Association of Investors Corporation (NAIC)
Madison Heights, Michigan
Copyright © 2003

First published in the United States of America by
National Association of Investors Corporation (NAIC)
711 West 13 Mile Road, Madison Heights, Michigan 48071
1-877-275-6242 • www.better-investing.org

Manufactured in the United States of America
Edition #1
ISBN # 0-9678130-4-2

Williams, Fritz.
    NAIC investing for life : youth handbook / written by
Fritz Williams for the National Association of Investors
Corporation.
    p. cm. -- (NAIC Better Investing Educational Series)
    Includes bibliographical references and index.
    ISBN 0-9678130-3-4

    1. Investments. 2. Youth--Finance, Personal.
I. National Association of Investors Corporation.
II. Title.

HG4521.W479 2003   332.6'0835
                   QBI03-200320

NAIC Registered Trademark Rights

BETTER INVESTING®
BI®
BETTER INVESTING BITS®
BETTER INVESTING NATIONAL CONVENTION®
BOND FUND CHECK LIST®
BOND FUND TREND REPORT®
BOND FUND COMPARISON GUIDE©
COMPUFAIR®
COMPUFEST®
COMPUFORUM®
CREATING AMERICA'S NEXT 50 MILLION INVESTORS ®
INVESTING FOR LIFE®
INVESTFEST®
INVESTORS CONGRESS®
INVESTORS EXPO®
INVESTORS FAIR®
INVESTORS TOOLKIT®

NAIC®
NAIC FIXED INCOME MUTUAL FUND COMPARISON GUIDE©
NAIC'S YOUNG MONEY MATTERS®
NAIC...Where Main Street Meets Wall Street® (& stylized sign post)
NATIONAL ASSOCIATION OF INVESTORS CORPORATION®
OFFICIAL NAIC MUTUAL FUND HANDBOOK©
OWN YOUR SHARE OF AMERICA®
PERT®
PORTFOLIO MANAGEMENT GUIDE®
SSG PLUS®
STOCK CHECKLIST ®
STOCK COMPARISON GUIDE®
STOCK FUND CHECK LIST®
STOCK FUND TREND REPORT®
STOCK FUND COMPARISON GUIDE ©
STOCK SELECTION GUIDE ®
STOCK SELECTION GUIDE AND REPORT ®

NAIC Better Investing Book Series

The Better Investing Book Series is designed to provide information and tools to help individuals and investment clubs become successful long-term investors. By using the series, investors will follow a self-learning pathway, gaining knowledge and building experience to make informed investment decisions. The series provides information and resources for beginners, intermediate and experienced investors.

For more information contact NAIC: 1-877-275-6242, or visit the NAIC Web Site: www.better-investing.org

Acknowledgements

NAIC INVESTING FOR LIFE – *YOUTH HANDBOOK*

Author/Writer:	Fritz Williams
Executive Editor:	Jeffery Fox, CFA Director, Educational Development, NAIC
Editorial Consultant:	Barrie Borich
Index Consultant:	Kathleen Paparchontis
Educational Content Consultants:	Richard Holthaus, President & CEO, NAIC Kenneth Janke, Chairman, NAIC Thomas O'Hara, Chairman Emeritus, NAIC Robert O'Hara, Vice President, Business Development, NAIC Jo Ann Linck, Secretary & Director, NIA Betty A. Taylor, former Director, NIA
Creative Direction & Design:	Michael Bell Sharon Flanigan
Design Consultants:	Ellada Azariah, Graphic Designer, NAIC Pamela Forton, Graphic Designer, NAIC Mary Treppa, Online Editor, NAIC
Production Coordinators:	Renee Ross, Childers Printing & Graphics, Inc. Jonathan Strong, Manager, Membership Development, NAIC
Printing/ Production:	Childers Printing & Graphics, Inc. Printwell Acquisitions, Inc.

Table of Contents

Foreword

Time is all-important in investing. Starting to invest when you're young can lead to substantial wealth if you establish and follow a plan — and if you adhere to NAIC principles of investing.

Following the first principle — investing regularly — takes discipline. It's easy to become sidetracked when everyone is predicting gloom and doom. Still, continuing to invest without trying to predict the direction of stock prices over the short-term will serve you well. It has long been my belief that to be a successful investor, you must experience a downturn in the stock market yet continue to invest. When prices turn positive, you'll look back and see that the bear market was actually a wonderful time to build up your portfolio.

The second principle — reinvesting dividends and proceeds from the sale of stock — taps the power of compounding. Examples in this book show how important it is to have the funds you invest earn additional money. The earlier in life you adopt the practice, the better your results are likely to be.

Investing For Life illustrates two key elements of successful investing — identifying the stocks of growing companies and buying them at reasonable prices. The greatest growth company in the world can turn out to be a poor investment if purchased at the wrong time. You must look not only at management but also at the price of the stock in relation to both its track record and potential.

Investing is a wonderful experience. It can provide a lifetime of success to disciplined investors — especially those who start early. I'm confident that if you put our advice into practice, you'll discover this for yourself and will be very happy with the results.

Kenneth S. Janke
Chairman
National Association of Investors
Corporation

Introduction

Money! Young people are making money and spending money as never before. When the school year ends, a second life begins, a life on the job. Fast foods, retailing, recreation, you name it. And with the money kids are earning, they are buying clothing, CDs, DVDs, tickets to shows and movies, and cars.

Maybe you are one of these young people. You are convinced that the things you are learning on the job are more practical and more interesting than the things you are learning in school. Or you may disagree and take the position that going to school is your job. What you learn in school will determine how much money you will make in the long run.

In spite of everything you are learning about making money, chances are you are missing out on some very important lessons about what to do with your money. There is a universe of money knowledge out there, and very few young people are getting a chance to find out about it—either in school or on the job. Kids know a lot about working and making money. But they do not know much about making their money work for them.

You may be surprised to discover that the real key to financial success is not how much money you earn, but rather what you do with your money. These critical money skills include knowing how to draw up a budget, how to prioritize your expenditures, how to save money in order to achieve your long-range goals, and most of all, how to use money to make money—by investing it.

That's what this book is all about. It's about money, your money, and turning your money into wealth. It's about the secrets of financial success and learning them when you are still young. It's about integrating these secrets into your life. It's about experiencing the power, confidence and independence that come from taking charge of your money.

Learning these secrets and applying them now will give you a head start. Saving and investing have a cumulative power. The financial gains are small at first, but after a period of time, they begin to add up. That's because you earn money not only on the money you invest, but also on your interest, dividends and capital gains. The earlier you start and longer you let your money work for you, the bigger the payoff will be in the end.

We think you will want to learn these secrets, not just because they can make you rich some day, but also because they will open up a new and wonderful world for you right away. You will discover how the financial world works and you will begin taking part in it immediately by saving and investing. You will gain a new understanding of who you are and what you are capable of becoming. You will put more lift under your dreams.

PART ONE:
A Life-Long Financial Plan

Plan Ahead

Chapter Goals–

After reading and reviewing this chapter, you will:

- *Appreciate the need for planning.*
- *Understand the stages of planning and be able to apply them in your own life.*
- *Comprehend the relationship between a financial plan and other aspects of planning.*

- *Be able to describe a proper balance between planning and spontaneity.*
- *Have a personal perspective on the relationship between dreams and plans.*

Introduction

In this chapter, you will examine the planning process. You will look at the stages of developing a plan and carrying it out. You will see how planning encompasses all aspects of your life and how these various dimensions of planning need to be coordinated. You will consider the tension between planning and spontaneity, and the relationship between dreams and plans.

Rule #1

"Which road shall I take?" Alice asked.
"Where do you want to go?" responded the Cheshire cat.
"I don't know," Alice answered.
"Then," said the cat, "it doesn't matter."

—Lewis Carroll, Alice in Wonderland

Life is a journey. It keeps on going and it confronts us constantly with forks in the road and unexpected crossroads. It is amazing and sad how often it does not matter to us which road we take because we don't know where we want to go. We live lives we have not planned for. We make life up as we go.

This is a book about setting our sights on a destination. It is about knowing where we want to go. It is about working on a plan for getting there.

Investing for Life contains a wealth of information on financial planning and investing for young people who are at an early stage of their journey. It is information which is not generally available to young people and which most people do not begin to appreciate until they are much older. But most of all, it is information that paints a clear picture of a destination for our lives and

revolves around a long-range plan. Before we can talk about money management and investment strategies, we have to deal with *Rule # 1*. It goes like this. *IF YOU WANT TO ENJOY A SUCCESSFUL AND REWARDING LIFE, YOU HAVE TO PLAN FOR IT.*

Planning is part of growing up. Young children rely on their parents and teachers to tell them what to do and when to do it. They follow a plan others have laid out for them. But as you grow up, you have to learn to do your own planning. You have to make up your mind where you want to go and then choose the best route to get there.

Again—*Rule #1: IF YOU WANT TO ENJOY A SUCCESSFUL AND REWARDING LIFE, YOU HAVE TO PLAN FOR IT.* Don't wait for the prize patrol to knock on your door. Create your own success. Design a plan and follow it.

Parts of the Planning Process

I. **A Goal:** You begin with something you want to achieve or obtain. You are not just living in the present moment, but want something more in your life, which will take planning, patience and discipline to achieve.

2. **Knowledge:** You gain an understanding of your objective and what it will require. You fill in the picture with research, conversation and thought.

3. **Alternatives:** You weigh your options, the different paths you might take to achieve your goal. You analyze the pluses and minuses of each–the costs, the demands, and the likelihood of success.

4. **A Strategy:** Based on sound information, the experience of others, and your own interests and abilities, you settle on a plan of action.

5. **Commitment:** You proceed step by step toward your goal. You keep your eyes on the prize.

6. **Flexibility:** You evaluate your progress and when necessary, you revise your plan to deal with changing circumstances and new opportunities.

An Example of Planning

This course focuses on long-term goals, goals that affect our whole lives. But to understand the planning process, it might be useful to see how planning works in achieving a very ordinary short-term goal: the purchase of a new stereo system.

1. **GOAL**
Purchase a stereo system.

2. **KNOWLEDGE**
Visit friends to hear their systems.
Study standards and specifications.
Check on dealers, brands, models and prices.
Consult Consumer Reports.

3. **ALTERNATIVES**
Second hand system– $250.
Pros:
Affordable high-end equipment.
Can buy right now.
Cons:
Uncertain condition of equipment.
No warranty or service agreement.

Compact shelf system– $325.
Pros:
Can afford now.
New equipment with warranty.
Cons:
Not suitable for adding extra speakers or using with television.
Not the best sound quality.

High-quality component system– $825.
Pros:
Excellent sound.
Greatest flexibility.
New equipment with warranty.

Con:
Costs more than prepared to pay now.

4. **STRATEGY**
Decides to buy the high-quality system, but rather than using a credit card and paying interest, will delay the purchase for six months in order to save for it.

5. **COMMITMENT**
Gives up going to movies for the six-month period, carries a lunch and stops eating out, places the savings in a stereo fund.

6. **FLEXIBILITY**
A model change sale provides an opportunity to buy comparable equipment for $600 four months into the plan. Makes the purchase paying cash.

Planning for the Journey of Life

No aspect of life is exempt from the need for planning. It is important for us to apply long-range thought, creativity and discipline to all phases of our lives. These include:

- **Career**–choosing a field of work and developing the knowledge and skills needed to enter and move ahead in that field.

- **Self**–deciding who we are and what kind of people we want to be, working to develop our strengths and overcome our weaknesses, refining our beliefs and commitments, a deeply religious dimension of planning.

- **Lifestyle**–expressing ourselves in the nature and quality of our everyday lives, our recreation and hobbies, how we use our time and money.

- **Relationships**–developing friendships and learning to get along with people in a variety of contexts, participating in family and community, nurturing intimate relationships.

- **Finances**–building the financial resources and the economic security that are needed to pursue all the other dimensions of our lives.

If we plan well, our goals and plans in these different parts of our lives work together and support one another. There is a sense of unity and purpose. This unified understanding of who we are and what we want to accomplish is not easy to achieve, but it is worth working for. This book is about financial planning, but financial planning works best when we know who we are and what we want in life, and we understand clearly why we are trying to build a strong financial structure for our lives.

Planning & Spontaneity

There is a natural tension between planning and spontaneity, between pursuing long-range goals and doing what we feel like doing right now. Any young person who has had to study while the rest of the family was in the living room watching television knows what that tension feels like. Anyone who has been invited to go to the mall to eat pizza and hang out with friends, but is staying home to work on a science fair project knows. Sticking to a plan is not easy.

Of course, planning and spontaneity are both good. They both have a place in our lives and we have to balance them. Having a plan does not mean that we are incapable of acting on the spur of the moment and doing something that was not planned.

Spontaneous events produce some of the happiest, most meaningful times of our lives. It is ironic, however, that those who do not engage in long-range planning and lack the discipline for it end up limiting their opportunities to be spontaneous. You are not going to play the piano at a party unless you have skipped some parties in order to practice. You are not going to travel to parts of the world you have always wanted to see if you have not saved the money. In the short term, planning involves sacrificing freedom and spontaneity, but in the long run, it enhances our freedom.

Dreams & Plans

Young people are natural dreamers. In their dreams, they are movie stars, criminal lawyers, and airline pilots. They are married to that certain someone. They are not simply writing an essay for a sophomore English class, they are wrapping up a column that will appear with their byline in newspapers in New York, Chicago and L.A. They are not shooting baskets all alone on an otherwise deserted playground, they are playing in front of a capacity crowd in the NBA or the WNBA.

Dreams are a source of pleasure. They are also part of making a future. If you do not have dreams or think that you are not worthy of dreaming, something very important is missing from your life and perhaps you should talk about it with a counselor. We all have a right to our dreams, and we need them—even if some of them are quixotic and fantastic and there is little possibility that they will ever come true.

Planning is not the same thing as dreaming, but it uses dreams as raw materials. It translates them into specific goals. It tests them. It lays out a course of action that moves us toward realizing these goals and sets up milestones we need to achieve along the way. Planning brings dreams down

to earth and turns them into something real and attainable.

DREAM: Becoming a trial lawyer.

PLAN: Analyzes skills needed and takes part in activities that develop those skills.

- Joins the debate club.
- Works with an amateur theater group.
- Participates in student government.
- Enters an essay contest.

Seeks more information on the profession.

- Talks to working lawyers.
- Reads about law in occupational manuals.
- Discusses requirements with a guidance counselor.
- Reads the autobiography of a famous lawyer.

DREAM: Going to Germany as an exchange student.

PLAN: Gathers program description and application materials and discusses them with:

> parents;
> guidance counselor;
> German teacher.

Works on improving academic and practical language skills.

- Saves up for and buys language tapes
- Carries and uses flash cards
- Starts a daily journal in German

One of the best things about pursuing our dreams is the fact that, even when we fall short, the effort leads to growth and opens a path to other opportunities. The young woman who practices the piano every day may not achieve her dream of becoming a concert pianist, but she may eventually put her appreciation of music to work as the director of an arts organization. A young linebacker may not make it to the NFL, but he may enjoy a satisfying career as a coach or a sports writer.

Without a plan, dreams simply dissolve. With a plan, they give shape and direction to our lives.

SUMMARY

Planning is a skill that is useful in every area of your life.

It is something you have to pursue consciously and thoughtfully.

When you plan, you translate your goals and dreams into step-by-step strategies, specific things you can do to test the feasibility of your goals and bring them to reality. You often have to revise your plans, but even when your plans are not fulfilled, planning will have a positive effect on the course of your life.

QUESTIONS

1. Think about your short-term goals. Pick out one that is especially important to you at this time and design a plan that includes all six parts of the planning process discussed in this chapter.

    ■

2. Select a long-term goal and see whether you can apply the six-part planning process to it.

    ■

3. Ask yourself how well you are planning for each aspect of your life named in this chapter. What sort of planning are you already doing in each category? What additional planning should you be doing?

    ■

4. What is the difference between a dream and a plan? Do you have dreams that should remain dreams? Dreams you ought to convert into plans?

    ■

5. How would you describe the balance between spontaneity and planning in your life? Would you like to shift that balance? How?

    ■

6. What is Rule #1? How would you explain the meaning and significance of the rule to one of your friends?

    ■

7. How would you defend planning to someone who says that planning is a waste of time because things hardly ever work out the way you planned them?

Developing a Career Plan

Chapter Goals–

After you have studied this chapter, you should understand:

- *Why it is smart to choose a career field as early as possible.*

- *Why you need to develop both general and specific job skills.*

- *How today's job market is radically different from the job market your parents faced when they were your age.*

- *How young people from ordinary families can afford college in spite of the high prices.*

- *Where to look for additional career and career education materials.*

Introduction

This chapter looks at some of the major issues in career planning for high school students. It presents a picture of revolutionary changes in the job market and reflects on their implications for future workers. It stresses the importance of training and/or education beyond high school. It suggests a "first class" and "coach" approach to planning for higher education.

Choosing a Career Field

Financial planning begins with a career strategy–a plan for weighing career options, making choices and preparing for your own field of work. The goal is to clear a path to work that offers good opportunities, that pays well, and that is suited to your interests and abilities.

Career planning is demanding, but it can also be fun. It requires an honest self-appraisal and an awareness of the occupations that match your talents and interests. Aptitude tests can give you a profile of what you are good at and what you like to do. You can also get a pretty good picture by reviewing your best subjects in school, your hobbies and favorite activities, your most satisfying achievements–and then asking yourself what all these things say about you.

Many school and community libraries have a career planning section with books, pamphlets and tapes on careers and job opportunities. The career Bible is the *Occupational Outlook Handbook* published by the U.S. Department of Labor.

It contains compact summaries of every conceivable job: nature of the work, required training, job outlook, earnings, related occupations, and sources of additional information.

It is tempting to sit back and let your school direct you into an academic or vocational program based on your academic record. But choosing a specific career goal as early in high school as possible has a number of important benefits. It enables you (a) to select the most appropriate high school courses, (b) to begin scouting universities, colleges, community colleges and training programs where you can continue your preparation, and (c) to seek out part-time jobs or internships related to your field of interest. Having your eye on a career goal can give a new sense of purpose and motivation to your high school studies.

What Employers Say They Are Looking For:

WORK ETHIC– promptness, neatness, positive attitude
BASIC SKILLS– reading, writing, math and reasoning
COMPUTER LITERACY– able to use computers on the job
DEPENDABILITY– able to follow instructions
TEAMWORK– works well with others
COMMUNICATION– adept at sharing information and ideas
RESPONSIBILITY– works well without supervision
INITIATIVE– applies knowledge in new situations
OPENNESS– eager to grow and learn on the job

Job Facts

Today's job market is very different from the one that awaited your parents when they were your age. In all areas, jobs are characterized by instability and change. Students are advised to set career goals as early as possible and yet to remain flexible and open to a variety of possibilities. You want to get on a career track. And you want to back yourself up with a solid all-around education in language, math, science and technology. Here are some of the basic facts:

Fact #1: The salary gap between low-skill and high-skill jobs is growing wider. As a rule, low-skill jobs pay poorly and offer very limited opportunities for advancement. A good job today almost always requires additional training and/or education beyond high school.

Fact #2: Education pays. The more education you have, the more you can expect to earn on every paycheck and over the course of your working life. In the following table, you can see that a college graduate earns almost twice as much as a person who only has a high school diploma.

MEAN ANNUAL EARNINGS OF FULL-TIME, YEAR-ROUND WORKERS 25 TO 64 YEARS OLD BY EDUCATIONAL ATTAINMENT (1997-1999):	
Some high school	$23,400
High school diploma	30,400
Some college	36,800
Associate degree (2 year)	38,200
Bachelor's degree	52,200
Master's degree	62,300
Doctorate	89,400
Professional degree	109,600

SOURCE: U.S. CENSUS BUREAU, CURRENT POPULATION SURVEYS, MARCH 1998, 1999, AND 2000.

Fact #3: Many of the fastest growing jobs are in technical fields that do not require a bachelor's degree, but involve a year or two of training beyond high school. At the top of the list are: computer support specialists, desktop publishers, medical records/health information technicians, physical therapist assistants, veterinary technologists/technicians, and dental hygienists.

FASTEST-GROWING OCCUPATIONS, 2000–2010
(BY PERCENTAGE; NUMBERS IN THOUSANDS OF JOBS)

Occupation	Employment		Percent change	Most significant source of education or training
	2000	2010*		
Computer software engineers, applications	380	760	100	Bachelor's degree
Computer support specialists	506	996	97	Associate degree
Computer software engineers, systems software	317	601	90	Bachelor's degree
Network and computer systems administrators	229	416	82	Bachelor's degree
Network systems/data communications analysts	119	211	77	Bachelor's degree
Desktop publishers	38	63	67	Postsecondary vocational award
Database administrators	106	176	66	Bachelor's degree
Personal/home-care aides	414	672	62	On-the-job training
Computer systems analysts	431	689	60	Bachelor's degree
Medical assistants	329	516	57	On-the-job training
Social/human service assistants	271	418	54	On-the-job training
Physician assistants	58	89	53	Bachelor's degree
Medical records/health information technicians	136	202	49	Associate degree
Computer/information systems managers	313	463	48	Bachelor's or higher degree, plus experience
Home health aides	615	907	47	On-the-job training
Physical therapist aides	36	53	46	On-the-job training
Occupational therapist aides	9	12	45	On-the-job training
Physical therapist assistants	44	64	45	Associate degree
Audiologists	13	19	45	Master's degree
Fitness trainers/aerobics instructors	158	222	40	Postsecondary vocational award
Computer/information scientists, research	28	39	40	Doctoral Degree
Veterinary assistants/laboratory animal caretakers	55	77	40	On-the-job training
Occupational therapist assistants	17	23	40	Associate degree
Veterinary technologists/technicians	49	69	39	Associate degree
Speech-language pathologists	88	122	39	Master's degree
Mental health/substance abuse social workers	83	116	39	Master's degree
Dental assistants	247	339	37	On-the-job training
Dental hygienists	147	201	37	Associate degree
Special ed., preschool, kindergarten, elementary teachers	234	320	37	Bachelor's degree
Pharmacy technicians	190	259	36	On-the-job training

*Projected. Source: U.S. Department of Labor, Bureau of Labor Statistics, Monthly Labor Review, Nov. 2001. Web: stats.bls.gov .

Fact #4: Jobs are less stable and secure than they used to be. Old jobs are being destroyed and new jobs are being created at a mind-boggling rate. Companies are attempting to keep their workforces lean and efficient. Lifetime jobs are rare. Workers can expect to change jobs six or more times, sometimes to totally different fields of work, over the course of their careers. This suggests a strategy that targets a broad career field and multiple areas of interest rather than a specific job.

Fact #5: The fastest growing group of workers in America is people who are working out of their own homes. They are accountants, writers, computer experts, sales people and many others who used to be on a company payroll, but are now selling their services to a variety of clients. Increasingly, companies employ people on a temporary or contract basis and it is becoming more and more essential for all of us to take an entrepreneurial, self-directed approach to our careers.

A Career Dilemma

Sometimes young people are caught in the middle. They know how important it is to earn a good income, but the work they would really like to do does not generally pay very well. They want to be artists or writers. They want to work with pre-school children or care for the dying. People are warning them. They are flirting with a career choice that may involve a significant economic risk or sacrifice.

There is much more to a job than making money. Between now and the time when you retire, you will probably devote more waking hours to your work than any other facet of your life. The happiest people are not the ones who are making the most money, but the ones who are doing work they care about and believe in. Their work is a labor of love. For them, work is a form of wealth.

Of course, money will always be important. You have to be realistic. If you choose a career that does not pay especially well, you will have to adjust your lifestyle expectations accordingly and you will have to do your financial planning around that reality. You may also want to plan a dual career—struggling to become an artist perhaps, but simultaneously providing a more secure economic base by teaching or some commercial utilization of your talents.

A good job is an important part of a personal financial plan. But a good financial plan supported by a lifelong investment strategy can also make it possible for you to do good work.

Career Information Sources

Occupational Outlook Handbook (2000-2001 Edition) developed by the U.S. Department of Labor, JIST Works, Inc., Indianapolis, 2000, with an affiliated Web site with links to other career sites. www.jist.com

Oakes, Elizabeth, H. (Ed.), *Free and Inexpensive Career Materials*, Ferguson Publishing Company, Chicago, 1998–a directory to publications and Web sites of organizations that provide free or inexpensive ($10 or less) career information.

Part-Time Jobs

It has become the norm for high school students to take after school, weekend and summer jobs. On the job, young people receive valuable workplace and money management experience. But there are also drawbacks. Most of the money goes into cars, clothing, entertainment and personal items, which may deliver immediate gratification and status, but have little long-term value. They are the opposite of what this book is about. They are not investments in the future.

Research indicates that jobs during the school year often interfere with schoolwork and that students with jobs may not do as well as students who concentrate on school and treat school as a full-time job. Academic success increases the likelihood of winning a college scholarship and lays a foundation for success in college–and that is more valuable in the end than all the money you could possibly earn in after school and weekend jobs.

In choosing work, it also makes sense for high school students to place more emphasis on career-related experiences, even where that means doing an internship for little or no pay. If you are interested in computers, you might want to pick up experience at a local company that does computer repairs and upgrades or offers networking services. If you are interested in television, you might want to work for a producer or television station as a production assistant. The pay may be more attractive at McDonald's or Burger King, but in terms of career development and total lifetime earnings, the career-related experience will be far more valuable.

Certainly, high school students ought to be putting a lot more of their money aside to contribute to future educational expenses and to begin the life-long investment program that is the primary subject of this manual. As you will learn in subsequent chapters, you might want to put money into a money market mutual fund to meet college expenses that are only a few short years away. And you could also begin developing a long-term investment portfolio that is based on the stock market.

Planning for College & College Expenses

Choosing a field of work goes hand in hand with selecting a college or training program, so as early as possible you should begin exploring your educational options. Ultimately, your goal should be to develop two or more possible plans of action.

Plan A, your first choice, should involve applying to the best colleges or educational programs you think you can qualify for. Although these may be private institutions that appear to be too expensive for your family to afford, you may be surprised to discover that a combination of financial aid options may actually make it possible for you to go there. Indeed, when you factor in financial aid, the differences in cost between a private college and a public institution may be much less than you thought.

Most of the many different financial aid programs for prospective college students fall into three main categories:

Grants and Scholarships

Aid you do not have to repay. Grants are usually based on need while scholarships are frequently based on academic merit and other qualifying factors.

Educational Loans

These are usually subsidized by federal and state governments or by the colleges themselves. Generally the loans carry lower interest rates than commercial loans and you do not have to pay them off until after graduation.

Work Aid

This is financial aid you have to work for, frequently 10 or 15 hours a week on campus.

Although financial aid may make it possible to travel first class, you should also investigate what it will cost to travel coach. There are many cost-cutting options: going to a community college for the first two years and then transferring to a four-year institution, attending a nearby college and living at home, enrolling in one of the 1,000 colleges and universities with cooperative educational programs that alternate between full-time studies and full-time employment, taking a full time job at a company that offers free educational opportunities as a fringe benefit.

College Cost and Financial Aid Information

The College Board College Cost and Financial Aid Handbook, The College Entrance Board, New York, 2001, compares costs and financial aid available at more than 2,700 four-year and two-year colleges. The Handbook also provides excellent general information on financial aid and a bibliography of other financial aid publications.

The College Board Web site, *www.collegeboard.com*, offers interactive materials for calculating financial need, registering for a financial aid profile, and a free scholarship search.

Informational Video

U.S. News and World Report: Getting Into College (c) 1998, 42 minutes, $14.95, available from *libraryvideo.com*. The video follows two high school seniors through the selection, application, and financial aid process.

Web Sites

FastWeb, a database where you can search more than 600,000 college scholarships and match your aspirations against more than 4,000 colleges. You have to log in, but the information is free. *www.fastweb.com*

FinAid, a guide to financial aid information on the Web. *www.finaid.org/*

Project EASI, U.S. Department of Education information on federal aid programs. *http://easi.ed.gov*

SUMMARY

To choose a future field of work you have to think about what you are good at and where your interests lie, and then you must learn about careers that use these talents and interests. The most rewarding jobs today require at least some education or training beyond high school, and your career choice should lead to a plan for preparing for that work by continuing your education.

QUESTIONS & ACTIVITIES

1. How do you make a good match between your talents and interests and a possible career?

   ■

2. Look up an occupation that interests you in the *Occupational Outlook Handbook*. What was the best thing you learned about this work? The worst?

   ■

3. Rate yourself on the nine qualities employers say they are looking for? What is your greatest strength? Weakness?

   ■

4. In your own words, explain the significance of the "fastest-growing occupations" table found in this chapter.

   ■

5. What balance are you trying to achieve between purpose and salary in your career thinking?

   ■

6. Using the *College Costs and Financial Aid Handbook*, identify the most expensive college or university in your state. The least expensive.

   ■

7. Using the *College Cost and Financial Aid Handbook*, see if you can find the names of federal financial aid programs in the grants, loans and work aid categories.

Managing Your Money

Chapter Goals–

By studying and applying the information in this chapter, you will learn some basic money management skills including:

- *Preparing and utilizing a budget.*
- *Limiting the use of credit and credit cards.*

- *Making strategic sacrifices.*
- *Becoming a more intelligent buyer.*
- *Developing self-provider skills.*

Introduction

This chapter describes five things you can do to manage your money better and make it go further. The suggestions are easy to understand, but it takes self-discipline and persistence to carry them out in your everyday life.

Avoiding the Earn & Spend Treadmill

Many people are on a treadmill. They work and earn all their lives, but never seem to get ahead. In fact, personal savings in the United States have declined significantly in recent decades. In 1998, savings dipped to minus .2 percent of income. That means the average American spent more that year than he or she earned! For some Americans, the erosion of savings reflects lower wages, but for most of us, the decline in savings has less to do with earnings than how we handle ourselves as money managers and consumers.

It has been said that we Americans are the most propagandized people who have ever lived on the earth. Every day, from morning until night, we are bombarded with messages telling us to spend money, even money we do not have. All around us, our friends and neighbors are obeying the messages. They are writing their life stories in red ink and they are encouraging us to do the same thing. Advertising is vital to the nation's economic welfare. But our economic health as individuals often depends on resisting the ads and making sure we buy only those things we really want and need.

When you are young, it is especially difficult not to follow the crowd and give in to the pressure to buy now and pay later. It takes self-discipline to resist the temptation of immediate gratification. It takes an independent spirit to see through celebrity testimonials and advertising images of the good life. You have to know who you are and what you want. You have to have your eye on the future. You have to believe in your ability to plan and manage your life.

Money Management Skills

If you want to exercise this kind of control over your life as a consumer and money manager, you will have to learn certain money management skills:

1. Budgeting

Budgeting means making a written account of how you have spent your money over a specific period of time and then using that information to give a more conscious and rational direction to future expenditures. It's a way of cooking and digesting the whole enchilada.

You might begin by tracking your expenses for a three-to-six-month period and listing these expenses in categories (see chart on next page). At the end of the tracking period, you can convert these figures into one-month averages. Then, next to this actual one-month budget, you can write an ideal budget that you will use to guide future expenditures.

Your final budget should have four columns: (1) tracking period totals, (2) one-month averages, (3) proposed monthly budget and (4) an actual month—to see how well you are doing in an effort to revise your spending patterns and make them conform with your proposed budget.

CHAPTER THREE

POSSIBLE BUDGET CATEGORIES	
YOUTH BUDGET	*ADULT BUDGET*

YOUTH BUDGET

Educational Expenses
- supplies
- special activities
- music lessons

Clothing

Other Purchases
- electronic equipment
- in-line skates
- CD's, books, etc.

Transportation
- gas
- car payments
- repairs

Savings & Investments
- savings account
- stocks, mutual funds, etc.

Gifts & Contributions
- presents
- church, charities

Entertainment
- movies
- shows
- sports events

Food & Snacks
- restaurant meals
- snacks

Other

ADULT BUDGET

Housing
- rent/mortgage
- insurance
- maintenance

Utilities
- heat
- electricity
- telephone
- other

Food
- market
- restaurants & snacks

Transportation
- payments
- maintenance
- insurance & registration
- gasoline, tolls, etc.
- fares

Other Purchases
- clothing
- furniture & appliances
- other household items

Medical insurance & Costs

Recreation

Savings & Investments

Taxes

Professional Services

Educational Expenses

Contributions

Other

There are enormous differences between typical youth and adult budgets, but the same basic principles apply. Drawing up a budget is the only way to get a reasonably complete picture of what is happening to your money. Often it will show that the little things are taking a surprising toll–and that your money is not going where you thought it was. The budget provides the information you need to spend your money more effectively and to bring your expenditures in line with your income, as well as your values and goals.

The budget enables you to compare how much you are spending on essentials and how much on discretionary items like snacks and nights at the movies. If you are interested in saving money for a major purchase, the budget will show just where you could cut back in order to do it. It will help you anticipate needs and it will reduce the likelihood of being caught unprepared.

Most of this manual is devoted to investing in the stock market. It calls for putting money aside on a regular basis, month after month, year after year. The way to do this, however, is to build saving and investing into your budget and to treat it as a normal expense—and not, as you may find in some budget plans, something you can do with your money if there is anything left over after you have paid your bills.

BUYING ON CREDIT

When we buy on credit, we are actually making two purchases: (a) the item we want and (b) the money we're borrowing to buy it. The price of borrowing the money is called interest.

2. Wise Use of Credit

The basic rule is simple. Reserve credit for special purchases and for expenses where it makes economic sense. Do not use credit for ordinary everyday expenditures such as buying food and clothing or paying for a night out.

You should probably limit your use of credit to the following three circumstances: (1) for major purchases such as a house, a car or college tuition, (2) for an unanticipated emergency or life-enriching opportunity, (3) for purchases where a retailer is offering an interest rate that is lower than the rate you are earning on your savings or investments.

SOME CREDIT CARD FACTS

- Although many credit cards offer attractive introductory rates, the average interest on a credit card is around 18%. *www.CasinoMagazine.com*

- Seven percent of high school students and 55% of college students have a major credit card. *www.hardnewscafe.usa.edu*

- Robert Manning, author of *Credit Card Nation* (Basic Books, 2000), estimates that 20% of students at four-year colleges have a credit card debt of $10,000 or more. *www.onlineathens.com*

- Many young people who are making minimum monthly payments on their credit card debts do not understand that only 5% goes toward paying back the money they borrowed (the principal) while the other 95% is interest. *www.hardnewscafe.usa.edu*

- Robert Manning has said that credit cards on the nation's campuses pose a "greater threat than alcohol or sexually transmitted diseases." *www.onlineathens.com*

- As many Americans find out every year, credit card debt has a way of escalating. Before you know what has happened, all your money is going into interest payments and you have no choice but to charge even more purchases. You are in financial quicksand.

- Still, credit cards can be useful. There are times when it makes sense to use a credit card instead of carrying a lot of cash in your purse or wallet. Credit cards come in handy when you have car trouble or an emergency on the road. Sometimes it is wise to buy a product with a credit card to give yourself time to inspect the item and make sure it is satisfactory before paying for it.

- If you pay your credit card bill within 30 days, there is no interest charge. You are simply using your credit card as collateral on your promise to pay cash.

3. Doing Without

It is ironic, but one of the keys to improving your status and achieving your goals is an ability to make sacrifices and give up, at least for the time being, some of the pleasures and luxuries others take for granted. Many of the most successful artists and scientists and people in a great variety of fields have endured tremendous sacrifices, especially early in their careers. They took these hardships in stride, hardly gave them a thought, because they were preoccupied with larger goals. In fact, they felt as if they were actually better off than their neighbors because their riches consisted of great plans and dreams.

Doing without may mean carrying a lunch instead of eating in restaurants. It may mean buying second hand instead of buying new—or in some cases, not buying at all. It may mean learning to appreciate public libraries, free concerts, and the simple pleasure of taking a walk. In the process you may discover that these are more wholesome and rewarding than activities that cost a lot of money. Learning to live a happier, fuller life on less is in itself a form of wealth.

The ability to do without can bring some practical benefits. It can free you from bondage to the present moment and the demands of present wants and needs–and let you look to the future. A determined pursuit of clear long-range goals and an ability to do without can be a very powerful combination.

4. Intelligent Buying

An important money management skill is knowing how to get your money's worth on the things that you buy–especially on food and other items you buy on a regular basis and on major purchases. These consumer skills include:

a.) planning your purchases and avoiding impulse buying.

b.) consulting consumer reports and other product information sources and making informed product choices.

c.) shopping and checking prices at different locations (i.e. comparison shopping).

d.) developing the art of creative purchasing—buying, second hand, flawed, wholesale, bulk, surplus, etc.

An intelligent buyer is in no hurry to have the newest product, the latest thing. The prices of many items drop significantly after they have been on the market a while and waiting allows time for the manufacturer to work out the bugs. The latest hit movie will soon be available for two or three dollars on video. The best seller will soon appear in paperback, and it will show up on the shelves of libraries and used bookstores. Cars last a lot longer than they used to, so it makes sense to buy used and let somebody else absorb most of the depreciation.. Excellent furniture, clothing and household items can be bought second hand. Wait your turn and save. The savings can be achieved with very little reduction in your quality of life.

5. Self-Providing

You can save a lot of money by providing in a direct hands-on way for your needs and the needs of your family. Do-it-yourself activities supplement your income, and they can be especially rewarding during the periods of unemployment and underemployment that are not uncommon in today's unstable labor market.

Home repair and remodeling can really pay off. When you save the price of a carpenter, roofer, plumber or painter, it is money in your pocket. And there are triple savings when these skills make it possible to buy a house in need of repairs at a reduced price. You not only save labor costs when you do the work yourself, you save on the price of the house and the interest that is included in the mortgage payments. In this way, self-providing can be an integral part of an overall savings and investment plan.

There are many other useful forms of self-providing: car maintenance; yard work; clothing construction and alteration; furniture refinishing; gardening; canning, freezing and drying food; furniture, musical instrument and electronic kit assembly; etc. Creating your own entertainment—parties, games, jam sessions, etc.—is a form of self-providing which should not become a lost art. Managing your own financial planning and investing, and bypassing brokers and advisors, is also self-providing.

Self-providing not only makes economic sense, it develops a more active and participatory involvement in the whole of our lives. Financial planning goes far beyond money management. It permeates every aspect of life. It is an important expression of who we are. It expresses a determination not just to accept our fate, but also to take charge of our lives and control our future.

SUMMARY

Budgeting holds the key to better money management and making your money go farther. It reveals how you have allocated and spent your money in the past and what you could do to make your spending more rational and efficient. Saving and investing should be an integral part of your budget, something you do on a regular basis and not just when there is money left over. The purpose of becoming more adept at handling money is to increase your ability to achieve your long-term dreams and goals.

KEY WORDS

BUDGET
CREDIT
INTEREST
COMPARISON SHOPPING
DEPRECIATION
SELF-PROVIDING

QUESTIONS

1. Find out what the interest is on the credit cards your parents have. How do those interest rates compare with the interest you could earn on a savings account? What does that tell you about credit cards?

   ■

2. Prepare your own four-column budget.

   ■

3. Can you remember any times when you put off or avoided buying something in order to achieve a long-range goal?

   ■

4. How is your family already engaged in self-providing? If you had to pay for those services, how costly would they be?

The Power of Investing

Chapter Goals—

In this chapter, you will learn:

- What investing is and how it differs from simply saving money.

- Why investing is so rewarding.

- How investing is growing in importance at a time when fewer workers are covered by company pension programs.

- How compounding works and delivers phenomenal growth to people who reinvest their interest and dividends and continue to invest over a long period of time.

- Four basic rules for taking advantage of the long-term power of investing.

Introduction

Congratulations! You are on to something. You have decided to learn about investing and to begin building your own investment portfolio. This is an activity very few young people even consider. In fact, most Americans do not become serious about investing until they are middle aged. As you will learn in this chapter, beginning young will give you a tremendous advantage and that advantage will grow over the course of your lifetime.

Saving & Investing

The term saving is generally used to refer to putting money aside for a rainy day, whether you stash it in a savings bank or a piggy bank. In a savings bank the money may draw a little interest, but that is not the main object. The point is to have the money on hand when you need it. Everybody should have some money in an interest-bearing account that can easily be withdrawn in a time of need.

Investing refers to something quite different. When you invest, you are not just putting money aside for a time when you may need it; you are taking measures to make your money grow. You are buying stocks or properties or anything you think will increase in value over a period of time. You are not worried about the immediate accessibility (liquidity) of your money. You are putting the money to work for you. You are using your money to make money.

As you learn about different kinds of investments in Chapter 6, you will see that there is no precise line between saving and investing. Investments range from money market certificates, which are a lot like having your money in a savings account, all the way to aggressive, high-risk stocks. Investing in the stock market involves risk. You have to know something about the companies you are investing in. But if you do your homework and invest wisely over an extended period of time, investing is a proven and powerful way of increasing your wealth.

The Rewards of Investing

1. Investing is a great way of making money. Too many young people think carrying home a paycheck is the only way of making money. Although they may realize that business ownership can be a source of income, too, they never consider the possibility that, by owning shares of stock, they themselves could participate in business ownership and business profits. They have yet to discover the art of using money to make money.

2. The rewards of investing can last a lifetime. Financial success does not consist of the stereo or the athletic shoes you can buy now. It grows out of the assets you build up over a period of time. Investing brings the deeper and more lasting rewards of security and economic power that come from the accumulation of wealth.

3. In investing, time is on your side. Stock prices go up and down. There are good times on Wall Street (bull market) and bad (bear market). But over the long haul stock prices have always gone up and patient stockholders can profit from that trend. In addition, investors who reinvest their earnings will see their money grow at an ever-increasing rate.

4. Investing can help you beat inflation. Prices have a tendency to rise over a period of time and we call that inflation. If our wages are rising at about the same rate as prices, inflation does not really bother us very much. We are not losing buying power.

Inflation does hurt, however, when you are saving or investing because the dollar you get back is no longer worth as much as the dollar you invested. If you put your money in the bank, for example, and earn 2% interest, but the inflation rate is 3%, you are losing money. Your money has developed a slow leak. Intelligent investing produces a larger return on your money than the rate of inflation. In spite of the bite inflation takes out of your money, you still come out ahead.

5. Investing is a way of owning a piece of corporate America. The money you invest helps companies buy the facilities and equipment they need to do business. Sometimes your investments provide the money it takes to turn a creative idea into an exciting new enterprise. If the businesses you invest in make money, you have a claim to a share of the profits.

6. Investing is fun. Sports fans never seem to get tired of trying to predict who is going to win the big game. Investors are trying to pick winners, too. Only the teams they are rooting for have

names like AT&T, American Express and General Motors. Sometimes investors, like sports fans, play a hunch. But if they are smart, they base their choices on research and reliable information. That is where this course comes in.

The Growing Importance of Investing

Jobs are changing rapidly. The old notion that you would work for one company all your life and then retire on a company pension is totally out of date. The world you are preparing for is not like that at all. Over the course of your career, you will probably work for at least a half dozen different employers, possibly in several different fields. Or you may work on a contract basis for a number of employers at once. With no single lifelong employer and no company pension, your long-term security will reside in your own hands. It will ride on your ability to manage and invest your money. Investing will not be a luxury.

The Magic of Compounding

One of the reasons why investing over a long period of time is so profitable is the fact that your earnings compound and as a result, grow by larger and larger amounts.

The concept of compound interest is simple enough. It is what happens when you earn interest not only on your initial deposit, but also earn interest on the interest. If you deposit $100 in the bank and earn 2%, you will have $102 at the end of the year. But if your account compounds annually, in the second year you will earn 2% on $102 and you will have $104.04 at the end of the year. At the end of five years, you will have $110.41.

When you study the Growth Rate Table, you have to be impressed with the fact that, although the monetary gains created by compounding are modest in the early years, they really begin to add up after two and three decades. At the bottom of the Table, the numbers generated by each dollar are growing by leaps and bounds. That is how it works. The payoff is huge for the person who starts early and keeps at it.

When you invest in the stock market, you make money in two basic ways–through the dividends which companies pay to their stockholders and by increases in the price of the stock you own.

Here, too, the dividends are reinvested and the stock price increases are based on previous increases so that the compounding effect is very real. How have stocks done

YEARS	GROWTH RATES						
	1%	3%	5%	7%	9%	11%	15%
1	1.01	1.03	1.05	1.07	1.09	1.11	1.15
2	1.02	1.06	1.10	1.14	1.19	1.23	1.32
3	1.03	1.09	1.16	1.23	1.30	1.37	1.52
4	1.04	1.13	1.22	1.31	1.41	1.52	1.75
5	1.05	1.16	1.28	1.40	1.54	1.69	2.01
6	1.06	1.19	1.34	1.50	1.68	1.87	2.31
7	1.07	1.23	1.41	1.61	1.83	2.08	2.66
8	1.08	1.27	1.48	1.72	1.99	2.30	3.06
9	1.09	1.30	1.55	1.84	2.17	2.56	3.52
10	1.10	1.34	1.63	1.97	2.37	2.64	4.05
11	1.12	1.38	1.71	2.10	2.58	3.15	4.65
12	1.13	1.43	1.80	2.25	2.81	3.50	5.35
15	1.16	1.56	2.08	2.76	3.64	4.78	8.14
20	1.22	1.81	2.65	3.87	5.60	8.06	16.37
25	1.28	2.09	3.39	5.43	8.62	13.59	32.92
30	1.35	2.43	4.32	7.61	13.27	22.89	66.21
35	1.42	2.81	5.52	10.68	20.41	38.57	133.18
40	1.49	3.26	7.04	14.97	31.41	65.00	267.86
45	1.56	3.78	8.99	21.00	48.33	109.56	538.77
50	1.64	4.38	11.46	29.46	74.36	184.56	1,083.66

through the years? Numerous studies estimate that the largest U.S. corporations (the S&P 500) have delivered an average annual return of 10% to 12% over the past seven decades!

To see the cumulative impact of an 11% growth rate over a period of 30 years, look at the 11% column on the Growth Rate Table. You can see that at 11% a $1000 investment will grow in value to $22,890 ($1000 x $22.89) at the end of 30 years. Admittedly, this is what you have before you subtract broker's fees and taxes and allow for inflation, but the result is still most impressive.

THE RULE OF 72

People sometimes want to know, how long will it take to double my money? Brokers and financial planners have a trick for figuring it out. It's called the Rule of 72 and it's a good way of measuring how compounding will affect your investment. Just divide 72 by your growth rate. Example: If the value of your investment is growing at a rate of 10% a year, it will take 72/10 or 7.2 years to double.

NAIC's Four Basic Rules for Investors

Based on many years of experience, the NAIC has developed FOUR BASIC RULES for taking advantage of the long-term power of investing:

1. Invest on a regular basis over a long period of time. Dollar cost averaging is a term that is used for investing about the same amount each month or so. When you do that you get fewer shares when the price is up and more shares when the price is down, and the net effect is a favorable average price per share overall.

2. Reinvest all earnings (dividends, interest, capital gains). Reinvesting your earnings compounds the productivity of your investment. You not only put the money you invest to work for you, but also the money you earn on that investment.

3. Invest in the common stock of good quality growth companies (or growth mutual funds). These are companies with established, continuous growth track records for at least five years and preferably 10 years. Rather than jumping in and out of stocks, you are looking for companies that you can stay with for an extended period of time.

4. Diversify your portfolio to reduce overall risk. It is not advisable to tie your investment future to just one or two firms or industries. You want to buy stocks in a number of companies representing different industries and different sizes.

A Hard Lesson

For a number of years in the 1990s, stock prices, especially Internet-related stock prices, made spectacular gains. People saw this as a chance to make money in a hurry and they violated all four NAIC rules. They did not pick stocks with good track records, but bought red-hot tech stocks on the promise of future profits. They jumped opportunistically from one promising stock to another. They engaged in impulse buying. Rather than diversifying, they poured their money largely into one segment of the market.

Unfortunately, many of these people entered the market when tech stocks were peaking and looking really good. It was just before the bubble burst. And when it did, they lost enormous amounts of money.

The investors who followed the NAIC rules, on the other hand, experienced far milder declines in the value of their stock holdings. These were merely bumps in a road that has consistently led to long-term gains averaging 10-12% a year.

SUMMARY

You are just beginning to discover the wealth-building power of lifelong investing. It is based on putting time and money to work for you. It is the art of using money to make money. By beginning young and investing modest sums of money on a regular basis over the years, you can produce very impressive long-term results.

KEY WORDS

SAVINGS
INVESTMENT
INTEREST
LIQUIDITY
BULL MARKET
BEAR MARKET
INFLATION
COMPOUNDING
RULE OF 72
DOLLAR COST AVERAGING
DIVERSIFICATION

QUESTIONS & ACTIVITIES

1. What is the difference between merely saving money and investing it?

   ■

2. What are some of the rewards of investing?

   ■

3. What is inflation and how does it affect saving and investing? How can someone earn 2% on a bank account and lose purchasing power?

   ■

4. Why is knowledge of investing becoming more important?

   ■

5. Describe compounding and how it works in your own words.

   ■

6. What are the two basic ways people make money from stocks?

   ■

7. What is the S&P 500 and what kind of returns have the S&P 500 stocks delivered over the past 70 years?

   ■

8. How long will it take for an investment that is growing 11% a year to double in value?

   ■

9. What are NAIC'S FOUR BASIC RULES for investors?

The Corporation

Chapter Goals–

After studying this chapter you should be able to explain:

- *How businesses secure initial funding.*
- *What a corporation is.*
- *The different rights and expectations of lenders and stockholders.*
- *The importance of limited liability for corporate stockholders.*

- *The difference between primary capital markets and secondary markets.*
- *The difference between a private corporation and a public corporation.*
- *The two different kinds of stock markets.*
- *What stockbrokers do.*
- *The "policeman" role of the SEC.*
- *The role of CPAs.*

Introduction

In this course, you are learning how to make your money grow by investing in the stock market. Each share of stock you buy is a certificate of ownership of a very small part of a corporation. Whenever you buy anything, you should know where your money is going and what you are getting for it. This chapter is devoted to helping you understand what a corporation is and how you can participate as a stockholder in corporate ownership.

The Two Basic Needs of a New Business

Whether it is General Motors or a plumber who works alone, every business offers products and services that satisfy consumer wants and needs in order to earn money. Businesses begin with an idea for a product or service and an interest in profiting from that idea, but before any business can begin to operate, it must meet two basic needs:

Labor Human beings who will do the work.

Capital Money to buy real estate, equipment and raw materials and to underwrite other start-up costs.

Sources of Capital

Generally, a new business needs more capital than a single owner or a small team of owners can provide, and it must look to two primary sources of business capital:

Lenders

People who lend money to the business in return for a contracted rate of interest or return for their investment.

Stockholders

Those who buy shares of stock in the company and, in effect, become part owners. Instead of receiving a fixed rate of interest, stockholders participate in the business and profit from its success.

Capitalism

The process of creating and sustaining businesses through private investments is called capitalism. Capitalism is very different from socialism where businesses are funded and owned by all taxpayers through their government.

Sole Proprietorships, Partnerships & Corporations

Many small businesses are owned by a single person or a small group of people, and they are legally organized as sole proprietorships or partnerships. The owners are personally liable for their company's losses and are subject to lawsuits by parties with a claim against their business.

In order to broaden company ownership and protect shareholders, many businesses are organized under state and federal laws as corporations. These laws stipulate that corporate shareholders have only a limited liability for the losses incurred by their company. The maximum amount they can lose is the money they have invested in the corporation. This means that some unhappy consumer who developed a hideous rash using a product manufactured by a pharmaceutical company in which you own two shares of stock cannot come after your computer, your ski board and your baseball card collection. Limited liability is one of chief advantages of the corporate form of business.

Private & Public Corporations

The vast majority of corporations in the United States are private corporations. Shares in private corporations are not sold on the stock market and can only be purchased from current stockholders—generally, a pretty small group of people. Private companies are a little like private parties. You have to be invited. Shares in a public corporation, however, can be purchased from dealers and trade openly on a stock exchange.

Primary & Secondary Markets

When a corporation is raising new money for some venture, it may sell stocks and bonds directly to investors. This process of raising new money and selling stock directly to the public is called a primary capital market.

As a rule, however, the stock you buy will be sold in a secondary market. A secondary market is created when stockholders buy and sell shares from one another on a stock exchange with the help of brokers. None of the proceeds of these sales go back to the corporation, which got its money when it first issued the stock. The New York Stock Exchange, the American Stock Exchange and the NASDAQ are predominantly involved in this secondary market of stocks and bonds.

When the economy is strong and public confidence is high, virtually any common stock can go public and trigger amazing price volatility. A good example is a new issue offered by Presstek Corporation, a laser printing company. On May 24, 1996 Presstek common stock was selling for $175 a share, a price to earnings ratio (you'll learn about this later) of 286 to 1. In 1995 the company's annual revenues totaled $28 million, but its market capitalization (price per share times the number of shares outstanding) was $1.2 billion. In a four-week period from May to June 1996, the stock price dropped from $175 to $69, based on disappointing earnings news. It was a decline of 60% in one month!

One form of primary capital market develops when a company "goes public" and offers its stocks and bonds to the general public for the first time. This is called an initial public offering (IPO).

The IPO market consists of many new and relatively small companies with very limited track records. IPOs are risky and often quite volatile (subject to steep price changes) and are not appropriate investments for inexperienced investors.

The Stock Markets

The two kinds of stock markets are: exchanges and the over-the-counter (OTC) market. Exchanges such as the New York Stock Exchange (NYSE) and the American Stock Exchange (AMEX) are auction markets where buyers and sellers come together to do business. The over-the-counter (OTC) or NASDAQ (National Association of Securities Dealers Automated Quotes) market is a virtual marketplace where the same business is conducted over telephone and computer lines. As a general rule, smaller and newer firms are traded OTC, although some well-established firms and a number of technology companies are traded on the NASDAQ as well.

Stockbrokers

A stockbroker is essentially a person who assists you in purchasing stocks and bonds. With few exceptions, most buy and sell orders on the stock market are handled through brokers, who serve as middlemen in the transactions. There are different kinds of brokers and brokerage houses. A full-service broker provides more hand-holding and investment advice, but charges a high-end fee. A discount broker charges less but may do little else than assist you in purchasing securities you have selected.

A broker's advice can be very useful, but you have to be wary. Brokers are usually compensated in commission fees and some brokers may try to pad their commissions by encouraging you to participate in more stock transactions (buying and selling) than are good for you.

The Securities & Exchange Commission

The Securities and Exchange Commission (SEC) is a federal agency that is considered the "policeman" of the securities (stocks and bonds) industry. The SEC is responsible for establishing and enforcing regulations that protect the investing public from unfair practices in the securities market.

When a company issues new stocks and bonds to the public, it is required to file registration information with the SEC. This information includes data on the company, its industry, competitors, management and other important facts. The company is required to provide full and accurate information. There are severe penalties for a company's officers who do not comply fully with disclosure rules.

Prospectus

The document that discloses financial information about the company and is filed with the SEC is called a prospectus. Usually, there are at least two prospectuses: a preliminary ("red herring") prospectus and a final prospectus. The nickname "red herring" points to the fact that the front page of the prospectus has red lettering to warn investors that this is a preliminary document. The preliminary prospectus does not include the price of the securities to be offered for sale. This decision is made on the day of offering. On the next page is the sample title page from a "red herring" prospectus for Dick's Sporting Goods, Inc.

Subject to Completion
Preliminary Prospectus dated September 26, 2002

PROSPECTUS

7,289,315 Shares

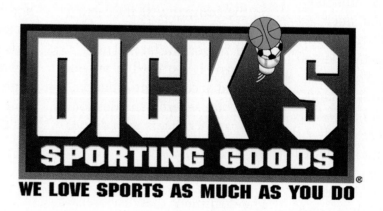

Common Stock

This is Dick's Sporting Goods, Inc.'s initial public offering of its common stock. Dick's Sporting Goods is selling 2,772,000 shares and certain of our stockholders are selling 4,517,315 shares of our common stock.

We expect the public offering price to be between $15.00 and $18.00 per share. Currently, no public market exists for the shares. Our common stock has been approved for listing on the New York Stock Exchange under the symbol "DKS."

Investing in our common stock involves risks that are described in the "Risk Factors" section beginning on page 8 of this prospectus.

	Per Share	Total
Public offering price...............................	$	$
Underwriting discount	$	$
Proceeds, before expenses, to Dick's Sporting Goods, Inc. ...	$	$
Proceeds, before expenses, to the selling stockholders	$	$

The underwriters may also purchase up to an additional 1,093,397 shares from the selling stockholders at the public offering price, less the underwriting discount, within 30 days from the date of this prospectus to cover overallotments.

Neither the Securities and Exchange Commission nor any state securities commission has approved or disapproved of these securities or determined if this prospectus is truthful or complete. Any representation to the contrary is a criminal offense.

The shares will be ready for delivery on or about _____ , 2002.

Merrill Lynch & Co.
Sole Book-Running Manager

Goldman, Sachs & Co.
Co-Lead Manager

Banc of America Securities LLC

William Blair & Company

The date of this prospectus is _____ , 2002.

Accounting

Publicly traded corporations are required to have their annual financial statements prepared by an outside accounting firm in conformity with generally accepted accounting principles. The statements are prepared by Certified Public Accountants (CPAs), accountants with extensive training who are licensed by the states in which they are doing business.

KEY WORDS

CAPITAL
CAPITALISM
CORPORATION
LIMITED LIABILITY
STOCKHOLDER
PRIVATE CORPORATION
PRIMARY CAPITAL MARKET
SECONDARY MARKET
INITIAL PUBLIC OFFERING
STOCK MARKET
STOCKBROKER
FULL-SERVICE BROKER
DISCOUNT BROKER
OTC MARKET
SEC
PROSPECTUS
CPA

QUESTIONS & ACTIVITIES

1. What is the primary advantage to organizing a business as a corporation?

   ■

2. What are the two major sources of capital for a business?

   ■

3. Distinguish between the rights and expectations of a shareholder and a lender.

   ■

4. When you buy corporate stock, where does the money go? Does it ever go to the company named on the stock?

   ■

5. What is the difference between buying stock in a private company and a public company?

   ■

6. Why is an IPO considered high risk?

   ■

7. What is the difference between stock exchanges and the OTC market?

   ■

8. What is a stockbroker? Why do you have to be careful in relying on brokers?

   ■

9. What have you learned about the accounting requirements for corporations?

The Investment Supermarket

Chapter Goals—

After reading and reviewing this chapter, you will be able to:

- *Describe the relationship between risk and return.*
- *Identify the factors that make certain investments high risk, others low risk.*

- *Name a number of investment opportunities offered by the federal government and federal agencies.*
- *Describe the risk/return profiles of various stocks and bonds.*
- *Explain how risk and return are weighed in making investment decisions.*

Introduction

For anyone just starting out, the world of investments can be very confusing. There are so many different kinds of investments to choose from. Where do you begin? How do you keep from getting lost? A modern supermarket contains an amazing profusion of products and brands, but a shopper soon learns not to search the produce and pet food sections for a loaf of bread. By grouping investments in categories based on different levels of risk and potential return, this chapter will help you find your way. It will help you form a better picture of the investment supermarket.

Risk & Potential Return

As you learn about investing, one factor you will encounter over and over is the relationship between risk and potential return. Low risk and a low rate of return generally go together, as do high risk and high return.

The relationship makes sense. Investments where there is very little risk of losing money can attract investors with a low rate of return. But ventures where the risk of losing money is relatively high have to pay more to persuade investors to take that risk.

Generally, buying stocks is riskier than making investments that pay a guaranteed rate of interest. Stock prices move up and down constantly and they go through periods (bear markets) when they decline in value. The risk of investing in stocks is not as great in the long run, however, and smart stock investors ride out downturns in order to take advantage of the stock market's general upward trend.

One kind of investment is not necessarily better than another. You have to choose investments

that suit your particular goals and circumstances. Usually what you want is a mix of investments that will help you achieve your financial goals at an appropriate level of risk.

The Relative Risk Pyramid

The Relative Risk Pyramid categorizes different kinds of investments according to their level of risk and potential return. It contains a very diverse assortment of investment options. Don't worry about understanding or remembering all of them. The object is to gain an overview of the variety of possible investments and their relative risks and potential returns.

Many of the investments in the pyramid consist of certain stocks or bonds—or mutual funds made up of these same categories of securities. Mutual funds provide an alternative to buying individual stocks. You buy shares in a mutual fund, which invests in a package of stocks or bonds. You'll learn more about mutual funds in Chapters 9 and 10. The main thing to keep in mind here is the fact that the same risk pyramid applies whether you buy individual stocks or bonds or invest in them indirectly through mutual funds.

(See chart on following page)

Level 1—Lowest Risk/Lowest Return

Loans to the Federal Government

Savings instruments and securities issued by the U.S. Government are considered risk free. They are guaranteed by the federal government, which has the power to tax and create money.

Series EE Bonds

The federal government issues savings bonds in denominations as small as $50, but discounted to be sold at $25. The interest on a Series EE bond is a variable rate based on 85% of the average rate on five-year Treasury notes. The major advantages of Series EE bonds are: (1) safety and (2) deferred taxes on the interest until the bonds are redeemed.

HIGHEST RISK & RETURN

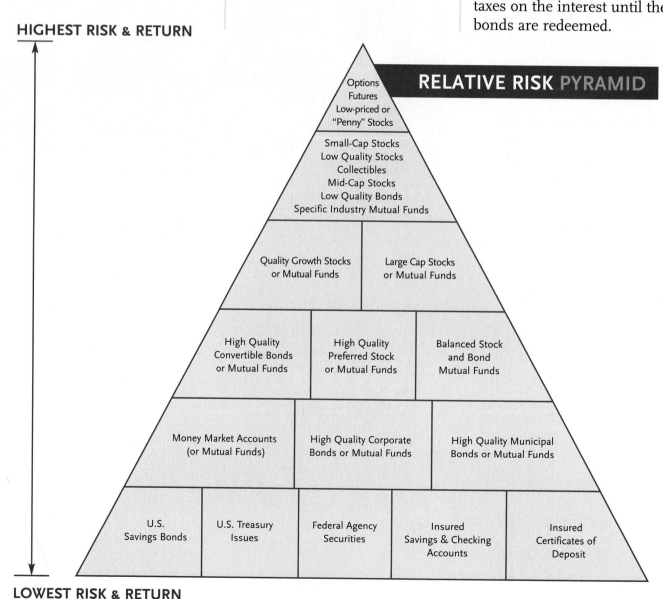

RELATIVE RISK PYRAMID

Options
Futures
Low-priced or "Penny" Stocks

Small-Cap Stocks
Low Quality Stocks
Collectibles
Mid-Cap Stocks
Low Quality Bonds
Specific Industry Mutual Funds

Quality Growth Stocks or Mutual Funds

Large Cap Stocks or Mutual Funds

High Quality Convertible Bonds or Mutual Funds

High Quality Preferred Stock or Mutual Funds

Balanced Stock and Bond Mutual Funds

Money Market Accounts (or Mutual Funds)

High Quality Corporate Bonds or Mutual Funds

High Quality Municipal Bonds or Mutual Funds

U.S. Savings Bonds

U.S. Treasury Issues

Federal Agency Securities

Insured Savings & Checking Accounts

Insured Certificates of Deposit

LOWEST RISK & RETURN

Series HH Bonds

Series HH bonds are similar to EE bonds, except for the fact that they are sold in larger denominations and at face value rather than being discounted. The interest on HH bonds is currently taxable. Conservative investors who want low risk and are prepared to accept a low interest rate buy both types of savings bonds. The bonds are non-marketable. They cannot be sold. An investor must redeem them, usually through a commercial bank.

Treasury Bills

T-Bills are short-term government securities sold in $10,000 to $1,000,000 denominations. Like EE bonds, T-Bills are issued at a discount to their face (par) value. They mature in 3-12 months. As low-risk securities, the returns are very low and vary in response to the overall interest rate environment.

Treasury Notes & Treasury Bonds

These securities have longer maturities than T-Bills. The notes mature in one to 10 years, the bonds in more than 10 years. Both are issued in minimum denominations of $1000. Because of their longer maturities, Treasury notes and bonds normally pay higher interest rates than T-bills.

Federal Agency Securities

In addition to the federal government, many federal agencies issue debt securities:

> Government National Mortgage Association (a "Ginnie Mae")
>
> Federal Home Loan Mortgage Corporation (a "Freddie Mac")
>
> Federal National Mortgage Association (a "Fannie Mae")

These federal agency securities tend to offer higher interest rates than the treasury securities, but they are still considered low risk. Treasury bills, notes, and bonds and the various federal agency securities are negotiable. They can be bought and sold in secondary markets.

Insured Savings & Checking Accounts

Most commercial banks and savings and loan banks offer checking and savings accounts which earn low rates of interest, but are fully insured for amounts up to $100,000 by the federal government (the Federal Deposit Insurance Company). Even if a bank or S&L where you have an account runs into financial difficulties, your money will be safe. Banks and S&Ls also sell insurance policies, mutual funds and other products, which are not insured. But checking and savings accounts are safe, low return investments suitable for short-term money.

Insured Certificates of Deposit

Insured Certificates of Deposit (CDs) are slightly longer-term investments ranging from three months to several years. The bank or S&L offers you either a fixed or variable interest rate over a determined time period. CDs are also insured for up to $100,000 per account. Because you are tying up your money for a longer time period, CDs pay more interest than savings accounts, but like other low-risk investments they offer relatively low returns.

Level 2—Low Risk/Low Return

Money Market Accounts (or Money Market Mutual Funds)

These accounts consist of low-risk, relatively short-term securities such as T-bills, large CDs and notes issued by large, stable corporations. Money market mutual funds are based on portfolios of these securities. Because these mutual funds are made up of low-risk securities and because the funds are diversified, they are considered safe places to park money for short periods of time.

High Quality Corporate Bonds (or Corporate Bond Mutual Funds)

By buying corporate bonds or shares in a mutual fund that buys corporate bonds, investors are loaning money to corporations. These loans are riskier than loans to the federal government, but if they are investment-grade bonds (AAA/Aaa to BBB/Baa3 as rated by Standard & Poor's or Moody's) the risk of default is still very low.

High Quality Municipal Bonds (or Municipal Bond Mutual Funds)

These bonds are similar to high quality corporate bonds, but with an important difference. They are issued by federal, state and city government entities, and the interest is tax-free. Municipal bond insurers guarantee a number of high quality municipal bonds against default, thus reducing the risk that investors will not get their money back. Municipal bonds only really make sense for investors in a high tax bracket, who have the most to gain from the tax exemption.

Level 3—Relatively Low Risk

High Quality Convertible Bonds (or Mutual Funds)

A convertible bond is a corporate bond that pays a fixed rate of interest, but can be exchanged for a specific number of shares of common stock in the same company. The flexibility has a price. The rate of return (coupon rate) is usually lower than the rate on a "straight" (non-convertible) bond.

High Quality Preferred Stock (or Mutual Funds)

The name is deceptive. Although it is called preferred stock, it is really a fixed-income security more like a corporate bond. For most individual investors, it does not make sense to invest in preferred stock because the yields are very close to the yields on similarly rated bonds and because preferred stockholders lack a bondholder's legal power to force dividend payment.

Balanced Stock & Bond Mutual Funds

A little higher on the risk ladder are mutual funds that offer an opportunity to invest in a mixed bag of stocks and bonds. You can even choose your level of risk. A fund with 75% of its money in common stock and 25% in bonds has a higher risk profile than a fund with 50% in each.

Level 4– Intermediate Risk

Quality Growth Stocks (or Mutual Funds)

Quality Growth Stocks are shares in companies that are leaders in their industry and have demonstrated consistent growth rates for both earnings and revenues in excess of 12%. These companies usually pay low dividends, but offer opportunities to profit from rising stock prices. Over the long run, quality growth stocks produce excellent returns, well above inflation. In Part Two, you will learn how to select quality growth stocks to invest in.

Large Capitalization (Large Cap) Stocks (or Mutual Funds)

Large capitalization refers to companies in which a lot of money has already been invested and which have a high market value. Market value is calculated by multiplying the number of common stock shares owned by stockholders times the current price per share. For example, a company with 100,000,000 shares outstanding at $50 a share has a market value of $5 billion—considered by many to be the minimum for a large cap stock.

Level 5– Relatively High Risk

Medium Capitalization (Mid Cap) Stocks or (Mutual Funds)

Stocks with market capitalizations that range from $1 billion to $5 billion are considered mid cap stocks. These are smaller companies that may have demonstrated high growth rates in revenues and earnings.

Small Capitalization (Small Cap) Stocks or (Mutual Funds)

These are stocks in companies with under $1 billion in market capitalization. Because many of these are small companies with short track records, they represent high risk and relatively high return potential.

Specific Industry Mutual Funds

When you buy shares in a specific industry mutual fund, you are investing in a number of companies in the same industry. For example, you can buy funds specializing in healthcare, financial services, technology or the Internet. If this kind of investment represents a major share of your investment portfolio, you are taking the risk of staking a great deal of your financial future on developments in one industry.

Low Quality Stocks (or Mutual Funds)

The definition of "low quality" is subjective, but these are high-risk stocks for a variety of reasons: small revenue and earnings base, erratic past performance, not being leaders in their industry, concentration on one product or service, market price of stock under $5 a share, questionable management, and/or the possibility that the stock is overvalued based on corporate earnings.

Low Quality Bonds (or Mutual Funds)

Because these are non-investment grade bonds, there is a higher likelihood that they could default and not pay the interest due and/or the face value of the bond at maturity. At the bottom of this group are the so-called "junk bonds." But term is deceptive. Some excellent companies are included in this group and their bonds may very well be upgraded because of improvements in corporate operations. There is a high level of risk, but low quality bonds have produced excellent returns over the past 10 to 15 years.

Collectibles

Collectibles include items such as rare coins, artwork and historical memorabilia. Collectibles are often used as investments by people who want to take advantage of their potential to increase in value over a period of time. Collectors need knowledge of the market for the items they are collecting and they must take appropriate storage and insurance precautions. You may have collected some baseball cards or sports autographs.

Keep them in a safe place and hold on to them. Some would argue that collectibles are high risk because they are subject to changing public tastes and can be difficult to market.

Level 6—High Risk

Futures

Commodity Futures are contracts to buy and sell items that are mined and grown–soybeans, coffee, cattle, crude oil, etc.–at some time in the future. The investor is betting on the future movement of prices, a speculative activity even for those who know the markets well. This is treacherous territory for a beginner. Beware of radio advertisements and telephone solicitations offering you an once-in-a-lifetime chance to make a killing in commodities.

Financial futures and currency futures are contracts involving future price directions of items such as Treasury bonds, Bank CDs, the NYSE Index, the British Pound, the Japanese Yen, etc. This, too, is a highly speculative area and is used by professionals for complicated hedging purposes.

Options

An option is a contract to buy or sell a stock at a certain price during a specified period of time. The investor is betting on the future direction of the price of that stock. Small price swings in the underlying stock will have a multiplier effect on an option's price. Large percentage gains or losses are characteristic of options. An option is a short-term vehicle used primarily by people who trade stocks. It is not for long-term investors, especially beginners.

Low-Priced & "Penny" Stocks

A low-priced stock sells for under $5 a share, a penny stock for under $1 a share. In general, these are stocks from small companies with no track records. In the penny stock arena, you may even find companies with no revenues and no earnings, only a corporation set up to pursue a future dream. Low-priced stocks are high risk. Although the low price may look tempting, beginning investors should avoid them.

KEY WORDS

RISK
RETURN
SERIES EE BONDS
SERIES HH BONDS
TREASURY BILLS
TREASURY NOTES
TREASURY BONDS
GINNIE MAE
FDIC
CERTIFICATE OF DEPOSIT
MUNICIPAL BOND
PREFERRED STOCK
CONVERTIBLE BOND
QUALITY GROWTH STOCK
FUTURES
PENNY STOCK

QUESTIONS & ACTIVITIES

1. Describe the relationship between risk and potential return and explain why they are opposites.

   ▪

2. Which government securities are marketable and which non-marketable?

   ▪

3. Characterize the risk/return profiles of the following investments: bank savings account, treasury notes, quality growth stock, commodity futures, municipal bonds, corporate bonds, balanced stock and bond mutual funds, small cap stocks and mutual funds. Check your profiles against their placement in this chapter.

   ▪

4. When should an investor play safe and when should an investor take on a calculated level of risk?

   ▪

5. What is a Certificate of Deposit? Why is it regarded a safe investment?

Buying & Selling Stock

Chapter Goals—

After studying and reviewing this chapter, you will understand:

- *The choice between using full-service and discount stockbrokers.*
- *The two kinds of analysis performed by investment analysts.*
- *The three kinds of securities orders given to stock brokers.*

- *The differences between a cash account and a margin account.*
- *The possibility of buying stock directly from companies in which you want to invest.*
- *The paperwork you can expect to receive after placing an order.*
- *The newspaper stock tables.*

Introduction

This chapter has two parts. The first part is an introduction to the process of buying and selling stocks. Later on, you will learn about evaluating and selecting stocks to invest in. But before you do, you will become familiar with procedures for placing, processing and confirming stock orders.

The second part of the chapter provides information to help you read newspaper stock tables. These tables contain concise up-to-date information on stock performances. Chapter 8 will survey sources of more in-depth information on stocks.

The Stockbroker

Generally, you buy and sell stock by placing your order with a stockbroker. Brokers go through training and testing to qualify for various kinds of securities licenses. One organization that administers proficiency exams is the National Association of Securities Dealers (NASD). By passing the exam, the broker becomes a registered representative of the NASD.

You can buy stock either through a full-service broker or a discount broker. Because discount brokers do not advise clients on stock purchases, but simply buy the stock they want, discount brokers charge considerably lower commissions than full-service brokers. After you have mastered the NAIC method for evaluating stocks, you should feel comfortable using a discount broker to place your orders.

A full-service brokerage firm usually has a staff of investment analysts who are assigned to follow various industries and companies in order to compile investment information on them. A full-service broker can provide advice based on these reports. In particular, brokers will tell you whether their firm's research indicates that a company's stock seems to be overvalued (overpriced), under-valued or fairly valued. The two basic kinds of investment research are:

Fundamental Analysis: an analysis of the company itself, its operations, its position within its industry.

Technical Analysis: an analysis of the company's stock, its price, price movement, trading volume, ect.

Let the Buyer Beware

A full-service stockbroker is a sales person first and an advisor second. A broker may sincerely want to help you achieve your goals, but in order to make money, brokers ultimately have to sell you products. As an advisor, a broker has a conflict of interest. In addition, because full-service brokers are paid entirely in commissions and make money only on stock transactions, they will often encourage you to buy and sell stocks when you really ought to hold on to the ones you have.

Even the advice of investment analysts has to be treated with skepticism. Analysts rely heavily on information they obtain by interviewing the managers of the companies they are following. Analysts do not want to lose these valuable contacts and as a result, they are reluctant to criticize corporate management teams. It is no surprise that analysts' buy recommendations exceed their sell recommendations by a margin of five to one.

BROKERAGE COMMISSION COMPARISONS		
TYPE FIRM	100 Shares @ $20 /share	501 Shares @ $20 / share
Full-Service (high)	$95.00	$248.33
Full-Service (low)	$65.00	$230.00
Discount – online (high)	$29.95	$ 29.95
Discount – online (low)	$ 5.00	$ 5.00
NOTE: TYPICAL BROKERAGE COMMISSIONS, AS OF FALL 2002.		

Because neither stockbrokers nor investment analysts are fully dedicated to the needs and goals of individual investors, it is absolutely imperative for each investor to develop the knowledge and skills to be self-reliant.

Placing an Order

Remember, we are looking only at procedures for placing orders. In Part Two of the manual, you will learn how to pick the stocks you want to buy.

You can place your order (a) verbally over the telephone, (b) through a touch-tone automated system or (c) by computer over the Internet. You will need to learn some of the buzzwords for the different kinds of orders:

Market Order:
You want to buy certain shares of stock at the best current available price and you assume your order will be executed as soon as possible.

Limit Order:
You want to buy or sell when the stock reaches a certain price. You will not buy or sell if the specified price is not reached.

Stop Order:
Your order to buy or sell at a specific price changes to a market order when the specific price is reached.

In addition to these three basic kinds of orders, you can attach a time limit to your order. A day order, for example, is good only on the day it is entered. When the market closes at the end of the day, the order expires.

Stocks are often ordered in even hundreds of shares (i.e. 200, 500, 1,000). When you order this way, it is called a round lot. An order that is not in even hundreds (i.e. 60, 128) is called an odd lot. It usually costs more in commissions to buy and sell odd lots.

Filling an Order

Because of the magic of computers, your order goes in a matter of minutes from your broker to the appropriate stock market. If the security you are interested in is listed on the New York Stock Exchange or the American Stock Exchange, a specialist there will handle your order. If it is stock in a company not listed on one of these exchanges, your order will go to a dealer in the over-the-counter market. On a stock exchange, a "specialist" does the actual buying and selling. When you are buying, you pay the specialist's asking price (ask). When you are selling, you receive the specialist's bid price (bid). The difference between the bid and ask is called the spread, which is how the specialist gets paid. In the NASDAQ and over-the-counter markets, a dealer handles the buying and selling.

Institutional Investors

Institutional investors do approximately 75-80% of all stock market trading. These include banks, bank trust departments, mutual fund companies, pension funds and insurance companies. Usually, they are large companies with professional staffs dedicated to investment decisions. Because of the size of their purchases, these institutions have a lot of influence on stock prices.

Types of Accounts

The two basic types of accounts with brokerage firms are: cash accounts and margin accounts. As a beginning investor, you should have a cash account, which means that you will be required to pay for your security purchases within three business days of your order.

Margin accounts are for more sophisticated investors, who are actually borrowing money to purchase securities. Sometimes margin accounts are used to conduct a stock transaction known as selling short. In a short sale, an investor acquires or "borrows" stock for the purpose of selling it and then pays for it at a later date—at the price of the stock on that date. Normally when we buy stock, we are hoping the stock we own will rise in price. But the person who sells short is betting that the price will fall between the time of sale and the time of purchase. Selling short is a high-risk, short-term transaction and is not an appropriate investment activity for a beginner.

Buying Direct

Hundreds of companies, including marquee firms like Coca-Cola and AT&T, now sell their stock directly and make it possible for investors to bypass brokers almost entirely. There are no sales commissions and the fees they charge are generally only a fraction of even discount brokers' commissions. For one-stop information and access to buying stock directly from companies, check out *www.netstockdirect.com.*

Documents on Your Stock Transaction

After the brokerage firm has executed your order, you will receive a confirmation statement. This written document summarizes the transaction—the number of shares of a specific security bought or sold, price, date, transaction fees and the amount due.

The securities you buy may be registered in your name or in street name, the name of your brokerage firm. If they are registered in your name, you will receive a stock certificate several weeks after the transaction date. If the stock remains with the brokerage firm in an account and the firm acts as custodian, you will receive a monthly account statement from the firm summarizing your security positions. Figure 7-01 shows a typical monthly statement.

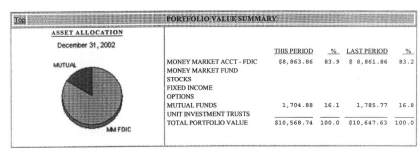

Figure 7-01

Reading the Stock Tables

You have probably seen the stock tables in the business section of your newspaper. If you have never used them–and most young people have not–the tables can look pretty scary, a sea of incomprehensible letters and numbers. But what the tables contain is a surprisingly simple, shorthand report on the status of the stocks traded on the different stock markets.

Part of the reason why the tables are difficult to read at first is the fact that everything is abbreviated, but the problem fades as you become accustomed to using the tables and you get to know the abbrevia-tions for the companies whose stock you are interested in. The sample stock table is typical of the general format you would find in local newspapers or national business journals.

Let's take a look at a stock table one column at a time and start making ourselves at home.

1. Hi: the high price for that stock during the past 52 weeks.

2. Low: the low price for that stock during the past 52 weeks.

3. Stock: the abbreviated name of the company.

4. Sym: the ticker symbol for the company.

5. Div: the current dollar amount of the annual dividend per share. The dividend is income paid to stockholders.

6. Yld%: the dividend yield of the stock as a percentage of stock price (column 5 divided by column 9).

7. PE: the price earnings ratio (price per share divided by earnings per share). In later chapters, you will learn about the significance of the P/E ratio in evaluating stock prices.

8. Vol 100s: trading volume, the number of shares traded that day in hundreds of shares. 1026 means 102,600 shares.

TYPICAL NEWSPAPER STOCK TABLE (SELECTIVE STOCKS) — JANUARY 17, 2003

J

52 Weeks Hi	Low	Stock	Sym	Div	Yld %	PE	Vol 100s	Close	Net Chg
17.61	6.78	JLG Ind	JLG	.02	.3	28	1022	6.90	-0.30
38.75	15.26	JPMChase	JPM	1.36	5.2	32	97668	26.19	-0.59
34.20	14.25	JackInTheBx	JBX		...	8	2586	16.52	-0.42
42.90	26.10	JacobEngrg	JEC		...	19	2493	37.87	-0.44
27.08	8.97	JanusCapGrp	JNS	.04	.3	8	7701	13.70	-0.24
27.95	8.25	JardenCp	JAH		...	21	1013	27.46	0.18
52.10	33.14	JeffriesGp	JEF	.20	.5	17	3020	41.10	-1.60
53.00	36.35	JeffPilot	JP	1.21	3.0	12	4505	39.84	-0.20
9.80	5.75	JilinChem	JCC		...	...	16	7.75	-0.15
33.98	9.50	JoAnnStrs A	JASA		...	13	2349	26.35	-0.20
40.90	25.84	JHancok	JHF	.22	.7	17	6181	29.44	-0.30
65.89	41.40	JohnJohns	JNJ	.82	1.5	26	55697	54.79	0.11

9. Close or Last: the price per share when the trading day ended.

10. NetChg: the amount the closing price moved up or down from the prior day's closing price.

In addition to the alphabetical listing of stocks on the New York Stock Exchange (NYSE) and the American Stock Exchange (AMEX) and major issues on the NASDAQ, you may notice summary boxes with items such as: top gainers, top losers and most active (in terms of trading volume).

When people ask, "How did the market do today?" they are asking about the average change in stock market prices. One of the oldest and most common ways of describing the overall performance of the stock market is to report on the Dow Jones Industrial Average and to note how these 30 representative "blue chip" American stocks did on a given day.

Unfortunately, the Dow Jones is no longer as representative of the total stock market as it used to be and it makes good sense to pay attention to some other more comprehensive averages or indexes: the NYSE Index, Standard & Poor's 500 Index, the NASDAQ Composite Index and the AMEX Index.

KEY WORDS

FUNDAMENTAL ANALYSIS
TECHNICAL ANALYSIS
COMMISSION FEES
MARKET ORDER
LIMIT ORDER
STOP ORDER
DAY ORDER
ROUND LOT
ODD LOT
NYSE
AMEX

NASDAQ
ASKING PRICE
BID PRICE
SPREAD
INSTITUTIONAL INVESTOR
CASH ACCOUNT
MARGIN ACCOUNT
DIVIDEND
DOW JONES INDUSTRIAL
    AVERAGE

QUESTIONS

1. Why should you consider a stockbroker a salesman first and an advisor second?

2. Why would someone go to a full-service broker? To a discount broker?

3. Why is it important for investors to become self-reliant?

4. Explain the concepts of fundamental and technical analysis and why both of them are important.

5. What are the differences among market, limit and stop orders?

6. What is a confirmation statement and what does it contain?

7. What information is contained in a newspaper stock table?

8. What is the Dow Jones Industrial Average and why should we pay more attention to other stock market indexes?

Stock Market Literacy

Chapter Goals—

After studying this chapter, you will be able to:

- *Explain why you need information to make investment decisions.*
- *Name the various categories of investment information sources.*
- *List the major corporate reports available to stockholders.*

- *Discuss why acting on inside information is illegal.*
- *List some of the most popular publications for investors.*
- *Surf the Net for investment-oriented Web sites.*
- *Benefit from television and radio programs with sound investment information.*

Introduction

Now comes the critical part of making an investment—finding the information you need and using it to choose securities. The investment process begins with acquiring information. The old adage "knowledge is power" is certainly true when it comes to picking stocks.

There are thousands of sources of investment information. Some are free. Others cost hundreds, even thousands of dollars. We shall concentrate on some of the major sources, many of which are available free of charge at your local library. The basic categories of information sources are: corporate publications, subscription publications and brokerage firm research reports. Increasingly, investment information is also available on radio and television and on the Internet.

The Need for Information

As a new long-term investor, you are interested in selecting and holding onto a portfolio of good quality common stocks. That means you want to choose the companies you invest in very carefully based on a knowledge of their past performances, their present management and their future objectives. You are not interested in a lot of short-term buying and selling, which would increase your transaction costs, but you do need to keep track of how your portfolio is doing in terms of achieving your investment expectations. In the following pages, we shall examine some of the better sources of information available to individual investors.

Information Provided by Public Corporations

The starting point is investment information provided by the companies themselves. Public corporations (companies whose stock trades on a stock market) are required by law to disclose financial information in various reports to their shareholders.

Here are the major reports provided by public companies:

Annual Report

The annual report is probably the most widely used source of investor information. Although publicly owned companies are required by law to send annual reports only to their stockholders, many of them will also send annual reports to non-stock-holders on request. The annual report contains an explanation of the financial results of the past year. But many companies also use the annual report as a public relations tool and a showcase for their products and services. An excellent booklet on reading annual reports, "Understanding the Annual Report," is available free of charge from the Chrysler Corporation. Below is a sample table of contents from an annual report.

The typical report starts with a letter to shareholders from the president or the chairman of the board of directors. It highlights the past-year management changes, organizational changes, dividend changes—and it may look ahead to the future and the company's future outlook.

ANNUAL REPORT TABLE OF CONTENTS

1. Letter to Shareholders
2. Company Profile
3. Financial Highlights
4. Operational Overview
5. Management's Discussion & Analysis
6. Financial Section
7. Management Report
8. Auditor's Report
9. List of Board Members and Corporate Officers
10. Shareholder Information

The 10-K Report

The 10-K is a report filed by a public company each year with the Securities and Exchange Commission (SEC). It is much longer and more detailed than the annual report to stockholders. Professional investment analysts use the 10-K report as the backbone of their research into company operations. The report is provided free to shareholders, if they formally request it, and may be provided free to non-shareholders.

Corporate Quarterly Reports

Public companies usually provide quarterly reports to their shareholders. These reports summarize activities in that quarter including unaudited financial statements. The 10-Q, a quarterly report filed with the SEC, is more detailed than the quarterly report to stockholders.

Other Important Corporate Sources of Public Information

Many companies publish news bulletins whenever a significant event occurs: an acquisition of another company, a merger, the sale of a division or subsidiary, introduction of a new major product.

Companies must file an 8-K report within 15 days of an event that could affect the value of the firm's securities. Changing accounting firms is usually considered serious enough to require filing an 8-K. If an investor acquires 5% of a company's stock, that person or that person's firm must file a 13-D report with the SEC. This report also alerts management that someone may be trying to gain control of outstanding shares.

Inside Information

Inside information refers to information that exists inside a corporation, but has not yet been released to the public. The securities laws of the United States forbid investors from acting on inside information.

Here's an example of an illegal use of inside information. Your brother works for a company that is in the process of being acquired by a much larger company. That information has not yet been released to the public. Over lunch, however, your brother tells you about it. As soon as you can, you contact your broker and buy 1000 shares in your brother's company. A week later, when the acquisition is announced, the price per share of your brother's company jumps 25%. It is the SEC's job to enforce securities laws. Using computers, the SEC discovers your well-timed purchase of 1000 shares. You face severe penalties including the possibility of becoming an insider in an institution that does not trade on the stock market—jail!

Newsstand & Subscription Publications

Many newsstand and subscription publications offer timely news and analysis for investors. While these publications can range in price from $15 a year to several hundred dollars a year, many are available free of charge at your public library.

Newspapers & Magazines

Your local daily newspaper probably has a business section with stock tables and articles about corporate activities (especially local firms). This is an excellent place to find stories about corporations that are located right in your own back yard.

In the investment community, *The Wall Street Journal* is one of the most respected sources of financial information. Published Monday through Friday, the WSJ is packed with a wealth of data and in-depth analyses of companies and industries. You already may have seen the *Journal's* "Classroom Edition" in your school.

Other trusted newspaper sources are: *Investor's Business Daily, The New York Times, Barron's* (weekly) and *The Wall Street Transcript.*

Dozens of financial magazines offer analyses of corporations, management and industries. The better general financial news magazines are *Business Week, Forbes* and *Fortune.* These magazines offer excellent lists and studies. For example, *Business Week* and *Forbes* offer periodic industry studies, comparing companies within an industry. Another excellent source of information for the beginning investor is NAIC's *Better Investing* magazine. This monthly publication offers articles on "stocks to study" and undervalued stocks, along with many helpful ideas for beginners.

Investment Advisory Service Publications

Hundreds of investment advisory information sources are available for purchase. Among the best known are *Value Line Investment Survey* and *Moody's,* as well as *Standard and Poor's Stock Guide, Bond Guide, Corporation Records* and *The Outlook.* The *S&P Stock Guide* and *Value Line Investment Survey* will play an important role in the stock selection process you will learn in Part Two.

With all the investment advisory services out there, how do you know who is reliable and who isn't? The publication, *The Hulbert Financial Digest,* provides monthly appraisals of the investment advice dispensed by many of the more popular advisors.

Brokerage Firm Research Reports

If you use a full-service stockbroker, you will have access to the research reports written by the firm's analysts. These reports may be several pages long and conclude with a buy, hold or sell recommendation. As a new investor using these brokerage firm services, you should be cautious about accepting their experts' opinions. The major advantage of the reports is the fact that they are free to the firm's customers. The commissions you pay on stock transactions absorb the costs. You should also note whether the brokerage firm is a dealer (market maker) for a recommended stock or whether the firm was an underwriter of any recent stock offerings for that company. These facts could influence the investment opinion offered in the reports.

Investment Information on the Internet

The Internet is a whole new frontier where investment information can be obtained quickly and conveniently, usually for minimum cost. The easiest way to learn of the many Web sites out there is to use browser software (i.e. Netscape or Internet Explorer) and possibly a search engine like Google to search for specific topics. New Web site information is being added to the Internet every day. There are some of the more important Web sites on the following page:

Looking for a specific brokerage firm or mutual fund company?

www.ml.com This is the Merrill Lynch Web site, where you can get the firm's daily market analysis and read about different financial planning ideas.

www.schwab.com Trading on the Internet is available through discount broker Charles Schwab.

www.fidelity.com Fidelity Investment is located at this site offering planning ideas, mutual fund information and brokerage service information.

www.vanguard.com This very professional site from Vanguard Group includes helpful planning tools such as an assessment of your investment personality profile. Check out the Investor Education section, which has a broad array of investment courses.

Looking for a directory of sites for individual investors?

biz.yahoo.com/edu/ed_begin.html Yahoo! Finance. It's a Web site of personal finance and investment Web sites and an investor's search engine.

money.cnn.com This CNN and Money Magazine site offers economic news and personal finance information. It promises to restore Pathfinder, an excellent starting point for exploring other sites.

Looking for investment information on a specific company?

profiles.wisi.com Corporate Information—you can read detailed analyses of more than 20,000 companies listed alphabetically with links to additional background reports.

www.sec.gov/edgarhp.htm This is the SEC's Edgar (Electronic Data Gathering and Retrieval) database containing the electronic filings of public companies.

www.hoovers.com This is Hoover's Online Database, which provides information on more than 8,500 companies.

Looking for general investment education information?

www.better-investing.org This is the NAIC Web site, which provides extensive services for Association members, both as individuals and investment clubs.

www.investware.com/aaii.stm This is the Web site of the American Association of Individual Investors (AAII) and it contains many helpful articles on the basics of investing.

Radio & Television Programs

One of the best-known investment information television programs is *Wall Street Week*, which airs on Friday nights on PBS. The program recently changed to new hosts and a new name, *Wall Street Week with Fortune*. PBS also offers the *Nightly Business Report* and a 15-minute *Morning Business Report* (Monday–Friday). CNNfn and CNBC carry extensive up-to-the-moment reports on the market and market discussion throughout the day. These programs are loaded with good information, but sometimes present this information in a manner that promotes more moving around in the market and short-term investment activity than this manual advises.

For radio listeners there are *The Dolans*, a call-in show with Ken and Daria Dolan (Monday–Friday, syndicated), *Marketplace* (Monday–Friday, Public Radio) and *Sound Money* (weekly, Public Radio). Broadcast times of many of these radio and television programs vary from market to market. For times in your area, check the local program listings or look up the shows or the networks that carry them on the Internet.

SUMMARY

Investment information is available in great supply. Much of it is free. In the future, more and more of this information will be accessible online. As a new investor, you need to know how to get this information. Analyzing a company is like putting together a jigsaw puzzle. After a period of time, when enough pieces are in place, you have a pretty good idea what the whole puzzle is about.

KEY WORDS

ANNUAL REPORT
QUARTERLY REPORT
10-K REPORT
8-K REPORT
13-D REPORT
INSIDE INFORMATION
WALL STREET JOURNAL
BUSINESS WEEK
BROKERAGE FIRM
  RESEARCH REPORT
HULBERT FINANCIAL
  DIGEST
BETTER INVESTING
INTERNET
WALL STREET WEEK

PROJECTS

1. Go to your public library and see how many of the news-stand and subscription publications they have. Skim through them to get a sense of their different formats.

   ■

2. See how many investment advisory service publications the library has.

   ■

3. Write for a corporate annual report and list the main sections of that report.

   ■

4. Contact a local full-service brokerage firm and request an analyst's research report. Check over it to see what approach it takes.

   ■

5. Visit several of the Web sites mentioned in this chapter.

   ■

6. For several weeks, watch one of the weekly television programs mentioned in the chapter with a parent or another adult who has some investment knowledge.

Mutual Funds

Chapter Goals—

After studying and reviewing this chapter, you should understand:

- What a mutual fund is.
- The advantages of mutual fund investing.
- The potential pitfalls of mutual fund investing.

- The different types of mutual funds.
- What an index fund is.
- How share prices are determined.
- What an expense ratio is and why it is important.
- Where to go for information on mutual funds.

Introduction

In this chapter, you will learn about mutual funds—and why so many investors are using them. You will learn about different kinds of mutual funds and how they are suited to different investment objectives. You will learn where to look for mutual fund information and some of the factors you need to consider when you are trying to choose a mutual fund.

What Are Mutual Funds?

Mutual funds offer an alternative way of investing. Instead of buying stocks in individual corporations, you buy shares in a fund, and professional fund managers take the money you and other shareholders have contributed and invest it in an assortment of stocks, bonds and other investments. In other words, each shareholder owns a small piece of the fund's entire investment portfolio.

As a shareholder, you are counting on the fund's managers to invest wisely. It is up to them to make money on the mutual fund's investments through dividends, increases in stock prices and capital gains when they sell stocks. After the fund's operating costs are deducted, a portion of these profits belongs to you. And as the fund's investments increase in value, so does the value (net asset value) of your mutual fund shares.

Why Are So Many People Buying Them?

There are several important advantages to investing in mutual funds. The first is diversification. It is not a good idea to own stocks in only a handful of companies. If one of them were to fall on hard times, you would lose a lot of your money. What you want is a diversified portfolio with stocks in a dozen or more companies including companies in separate industries. A severe decline in one stock would be balanced by the performance of others. It is not unusual for a mutual fund to hold stocks in 100 or more different companies.

The second advantage of mutual funds is professional fund management. Many individual investors do not feel secure about investing directly in the stock market. They do not have the knowledge or dedication it takes to choose and track individual stocks. In a mutual fund, experienced full-time

---

Mutual Fund Prices & Net Asset Value (NAV)

Unlike stocks, most mutual fund prices are not determined by what people are willing to pay for them at a given time. They are determined by the total value of a fund's investment portfolio minus liabilities divided by the number of shares outstanding. Net asset value is calculated at the end of each business day!

Portfolio Value – Liabilities / Shares = NAV

Shareholder
$
buys shares

↓

Mutual Fund
makes investments

↓

Stocks & Other Investments

Stocks & Other Investments
$
pay dividends
increase in price
produce capital gains

↓

Mutual Fund
passes on dividends
value of shares increases

↓

Shareholder

managers and analysts handle your investments. These investment professionals are compensated through the management fees, which are part of the fund's operating expenses.

The third advantage is convenience. Mutual funds are easy to buy and sell. You can conduct mutual fund transactions through a brokerage firm, a bank or the mutual fund company itself. You can obtain a prospectus and an application from a fund by calling a toll-free number or by visiting the fund's Web site and downloading the materials by computer. Then, you mail the completed application and enclose a check to cover your purchase.

If you own shares in a fund that belongs to a family of funds (funds managed by the same company) you can transfer from one fund to another whenever your investment needs or goals change. Mutual funds also offer the option of automatic reinvestment of dividends and capital gains and they allow you to arrange for monthly payment deductions from a bank account.

The Mutual Fund Universe

Mutual funds have become very popular and they account for much of the stock market's phenomenal growth in the past decade. But people who think that mutual funds are an easy ride had better be careful. Mutual funds have their winners and losers just like stocks, and as we shall observe later, professional fund management is no guarantee of success.

There are now thousands of mutual funds representing a variety of investments and objectives. That means you have to be clear about your investment goals and the level of risk you are willing to accept if you want to choose a fund that is right for you. You may choose Fund A because you are interested in secure short-term income—or Fund B because you are prepared to take some risks in order to achieve more dramatic long-term growth.

Then, after you have chosen the type of fund you want, examine specific funds in that category very carefully before you buy. Compare their performance records, their management, and the growth and income potential of their investment portfolios. Buying a mutual fund is not all that different from buying stock. You have to do your homework.

You begin to get some idea of the complexity of mutual fund investing when you look at how the funds are grouped into categories based on the investments they make and their overall objectives. For example, here is one way of grouping them:

- Common stock funds
- Balanced funds (stocks and bonds)
- Municipal (tax exempt) bond funds
- Corporate bond funds
- Government bond funds
- Money market funds

The stock market funds provide the greatest growth potential and carry the greatest risk. Within the stock funds, however, there are some important subdivisions:

- Aggressive growth (small companies with high growth potential)
- Long-term growth (better known steady-growth firms)
- Growth and income (a mixed portfolio of stocks and bonds)
- Value funds (stocks which are down, but have potential for recovery)
- Sector funds (stocks from one industrial sector)
- International funds (stocks from other parts of the world).

Sometimes the names of mutual funds let you know what kinds of funds they are: T. Rowe Price Equity Income Fund (mix of stocks and bonds), Montgomery Small Cap Fund (aggressive growth), Fidelity Utilities Fund (sector). But often (The New America Fund, The New Era Fund) you need to examine a prospectus or a profile to find out.

Lighten the Load

All funds incur administrative and managerial costs and investors must be prepared to pay certain charges to cover them. Still, the object should be to keep these charges as low as possible. Load funds charge an up-front sales commission or "load," but plenty of no-load funds charge no sales fee. Upfront charges are costly. An 8% load on a $10,000 investment means that you are really investing only $9,200. Some people buy load funds in order to obtain the assistance of a financial advisor. We think people should learn to make their own mutual fund decisions.

In addition to upfront loads or charges, a number of other fees are commonly associated with mutual funds. Lumped together, these operating expenses are usually expressed as a percentage (or expense ratio) of your total investment. Expense ratios range from approximately .18 to 5%. We suggest you review thoroughly funds with expense ratios higher than 1.5%.

Operating expenses have a dramatic impact on the long-term performance of a fund. Here is an example of how significant that impact can be:

	Fund A	Fund B
Expense ratio	0.45%	2.1%
Value of $10,000 in 20 years	$61,979	$45,754

(Assumes 10% annualized total return before operating expenses)

Index Funds

Index funds are a special category of mutual funds that have recently become very popular. Instead of offering portfolios of professionally selected stocks as most mutual funds do, an index fund simply invests in a representative sample of the entire stock market or a market segment (utilities, communications, pharmaceuticals, etc.).

There is good reason for the popularity of index funds. Because index funds do not involve professional analysts and managers, administrative and managerial costs are generally low. And because buying and selling stock within a fund is minimized, transaction costs and capital gains taxes are also relatively low.

You would think that managed funds would compensate for these disadvantages by outperforming index funds—and maybe they will in more difficult economic times, but in the extended bull market of the 1990s, most professionally managed funds did not outperform the S&P 500 index of stocks and the stock market in general.

Getting the Low Down

You can follow the progress of mutual funds, just like stocks, in many local newspapers. Some papers publish an "expanded table" of mutual funds one day of the week. *The Wall Street Journal* publishes an expanded table of mutual funds on a monthly basis.

Newspaper tables are great for a quick overview of mutual funds and how they are performing, but if you want to invest in them, you will also need to use an indepth information source such as:

Morningstar Mutual Funds

Morningstar is available on a subscription basis and it is also found in the reference section of many public libraries. In a compact one-page presentation, *Morningstar* displays a wealth of information on a specific fund. Using *Morningstar* you can evaluate the fund's performance over a 10-year period, examine its investment portfolio and assess its risks. The next chapter shows how to use *Morningstar* reports to compare various funds.

Standard & Poor's/Lipper Mutual Fund Profiles

This mutual fund source is also available by subscription and at many public libraries. The *S&P/Lipper Report* is a half-page summary with the following information: industry percentages, top holdings, performance data, expenses and fees.

Magazines

Forbes magazine publishes a mutual fund issue in August each year. The larger, more popular funds are grouped by investment objectives. Performance data are available, with the added feature of ratings of fund performances in up-and-down markets. The *Forbes* mutual fund issue also contains sales charge and operating expense information. *Forbes* is probably available in your local library.

Another survey of 2,500 mutual funds is found in *Money* magazine. The information includes: type of fund, style of investing, risk level, annualized total returns for up to 10 years, sales loads, annual fees, size of portfolio and the fund's telephone number.

Business Week magazine publishes a quarterly "Mutual Fund Scorecard," which has performance data on more than 700 funds. The Scorecard also contains: investment objectives, turnover, sales charges, operating fees, percent in cash and largest stock holdings. Your local library should have the magazine. The data is also available on diskette.

Other publications with mutual fund performance information are *Barron's, Fortune, Fw, Kiplinger's Personal Finance* and *Consumer Reports*.

Radio

Bob Brinker's Moneytalk airs nationwide on ABC radio network stations on Saturdays and Sundays from 4 p.m. to 7 p.m. ET. Brinker is an advocate of informed, no-load, balanced portfolio, dollar-cost-averaged mutual fund investing.

Internet Information Sources

www.better-investing.org/funds NAIC's Mutual Fund Education and Resource Center provides you access to all of NAIC's mutual fund tools, data, analysis and education.

Quicken.com and *mfea.com* (Mutual Fund Educational Alliance) are online investing centers where users can look up funds by families and categories and compare recent performances with performances over the past three and five years. Both sites also provide means for obtaining prices, prospectuses and application forms. *Quicken.com* (click on brokerage, then funds) has guidance for searching for funds that meet individual investment needs and criteria. *Mfea.com* has educational information for novice and more seasoned investors along with news and commentary on mutual funds.

Morningstar *(morningstar.com)* offers a "portfolio x-ray" enabling investors to examine the funds they own in greater depth. The x-ray looks at sectors, regions, company sizes and P/E ratios of the stock held by various mutual funds and helps investors assemble stronger, better-balanced portfolios.

Bobbrinker.com contains mutual fund information from his syndicated radio show and his subscription newsletter, together with a topical manual for new mutual fund investors.

Investing for Beginners *(beginnersinvest.about.com)* has investing lessons for beginners with a section on mutual fund basics and links to mutual fund company sites.

Brill.com is an interactive site where investors react to recent events affecting the market and the changing investment climate.

SUMMARY

Mutual funds provide a practical way for ordinary investors to participate in the stock market. Mutual funds may be used as an alternative to investing in individual stocks or they may be used to complement and diversify a stock portfolio. There are many different kinds of mutual funds with a wide range of stock, bond and money market portfolios and a variety of investment goals. Intelligent mutual fund investors select fund categories that match their investment objectives. Then, they carefully evaluate the performance record, portfolio, management, the costs, and the growth and income potential of individual funds before they invest. An NAIC program for evaluating mutual funds is presented in the next chapter.

KEY WORDS

MUTUAL FUND
PROFESSIONAL MANAGER
PORTFOLIO DIVERSIFICATION
NET ASSET VALUE
AGGRESSIVE GROWTH FUND
GROWTH AND INCOME
  FUND

INDEX FUND
SECTOR FUND
NO-LOAD FUND
OPERATING EXPENSES
EXPENSE RATIO
MORNINGSTAR

QUESTIONS & ACTIVITIES

1. What are mutual funds and why are they so popular?

   ■

2. What are the main categories of mutual funds? Which involve the highest risk and offer the highest growth potential?

   ■

3. What is an index fund? Why are many people choosing index funds today?

   ■

4. What are some mistakes mutual fund investors must avoid?

   ■

5. How are mutual fund prices determined? What does NAV stand for and how is it calculated?

   ■

6. What is a fund's expense ratio and why is it important?

   ■

7. Surf the Net! Find the site that tells you about the top 25 aggressive growth stock funds. Using *mfea.com*, visit a mutual fund family Web site and examine prospectus and application materials.

Selecting Mutual Funds

Chapter Goals—

After studying and reviewing this chapter, you should understand:

- *The key elements of a mutual fund.*
- *NAIC's three mutual fund analysis tools.*

- *The importance of fund management.*
- *How costs impact fund returns.*

Introduction

NAIC's mutual fund program provides you with the tools you need to select mutual funds that fit into your financial plan. With thousands of funds competing for your attention, it's difficult to figure out which funds merit consideration.

As an investor it is necessary for you to determine whether the investment you're considering is a good quality investment that you feel confident will increase in value over time.

The program's three Stock Fund tools —the Stock Fund Check List, Stock Fund Comparison Guide and Stock Fund Trend Report—enable you to find such investments.

NAIC Mutual Fund Tools

The NAIC mutual fund program is built around three tools:

- The Stock Fund Check List, a one-page, two-sided form designed to help you analyze one fund.

- The Stock Fund Comparison Guide, a one-page, one-sided form allows you to compare the key elements of several funds.

- The Stock Fund Trend Report, a one-page, one-sided form designed so you can track the important character- istics of a fund you own.

Each tool draws basic information about a mutual fund's portfolio, management and costs using data found on Morningstar reports. The Morningstar report for the Dreyfus Appreciation Fund is included on Page 64 so you can see what a report looks like. We've also provided part of the Check List form.

The Fund Selection Process

The selection process begins with gathering basic information about a fund. NAIC designed its mutual fund program to cut through the confusion to create a sound basis for choosing a fund.

Find out what a fund's minimum purchase requirement is. No matter how wonderful a fund is, if it requires more of an initial investment than you can afford, there is no reason to investigate it further. Many funds either have low minimum

investment requirements or offer automatic investment programs where you can invest as little as $25 or $50 a month.

Look at a fund's investment objective to see if it is in line with your investment objective. Make sure that a fund's portfolio holdings follow this investment objective. When you purchase shares in a mutual fund, you employ a portfolio manager to invest your money for you. Look for a portfolio manager who has been with a fund for

Data through June 30, 2002

Dreyfus Appreciation

	Ticker	Load	NAV	Yield	Total Assets	Mstar Category
	DGAGX	None	$34.59	0.8%	$3,259 mil	Large Blend

Manager Strategy

This fund is one of many plays on blue-chip names, but management's preference for companies with proven and well-known brands separates it from the pack. Thus, it holds more consumer-goods companies and fewer technology names than the typical large-blend fund. It's also more concentrated in individual issues. Management takes a buy-and-hold approach, as is reflected in the fund's miniscule turnover ratio, which in turn translates into strong tax-efficiency marks.

Historical Profile

Return	Above Avg
Risk	Below Avg
Rating	★★★★ Above Avg

Investment Style
Equity
Stock %

▼ Manager Change
▽ Partial Manager Change

Fund Performance vs. Category Average.
  Quarterly Fund Return
  +/- Category Average
— Category Baseline

Performance Quartile (within Category)

Portfolio Manager(s)

Fayez Sarofim. Since 12-90. BS U. of California-Berkeley; MBA Harvard U. Other funds currently managed: Dreyfus Premier Worldwide Growth T, Dreyfus Premier Core Equity A, Dreyfus Premier Tax-Managed Growth A.

1991	1992	1993	1994	1995	1996	1997	1998	1999	2000	2001	06-02	History
14.67	15.15	14.92	15.17	20.55	25.58	32.38	42.07	45.73	42.94	38.02	34.59	NAV
38.43	4.28	0.71	3.62	37.89	25.67	27.85	30.85	9.97	1.80	-10.75	-8.98	Total Return %
7.95	-3.34	-9.35	2.31	0.35	2.73	2.27	-11.07	10.90	1.13	4.17	—	+/-S&P 500
5.99	-3.37	-9.13	3.17	0.29	3.51	-5.17	2.22	-11.86	12.76	2.02	3.83	+/-Wilshire Lrg 750
1.83	0.68	1.77	1.86	2.21	1.22	1.02	0.70	0.55	0.63	0.71	0.00	Income Return %
36.60	3.60	-1.06	1.76	35.68	24.45	26.83	30.15	9.42	1.17	-11.46	-8.98	Capital Return %
21	83	98	8	13	9	53	9	87	16	28	14	Total Rtn % Rank Cat
0.20	0.10	0.27	0.28	0.34	0.25	0.26	0.23	0.23	0.29	0.31	0.00	Income $
0.25	0.05	0.06	0.01	0.03	0.00	0.06	0.07	0.31	3.22	0.00	0.02	Capital Gains $
1.30	1.14	1.07	0.96	0.92	0.91	0.87	0.89	0.87	0.88	0.91	—	Expense Ratio %
1.69	1.46	1.66	1.86	2.28	1.34	0.99	0.75	0.51	0.64	0.72	—	Income Ratio %
13	3	10	7	5	1	1	1	12	4	5	—	Turnover Rate %
81	208	237	234	461	877	1,979	4,169	4,751	3,854	3,427	3,259	Net Assets $mil

Performance 06-30-02

	1st Qtr	2nd Qtr	3rd Qtr	4th Qtr	Total
1998	15.69	4.54	-10.23	20.52	30.85
1999	3.12	3.64	-6.65	10.22	9.97
2000	0.65	2.94	-1.98	0.24	1.80
2001	-10.83	3.79	-8.74	5.67	-10.75
2002	2.60	-11.28	—	—	—

Trailing	Total Return%	+/- S&P 500	+/- Wilshire Lrg 750	%Rank All Cat	Growth of $10,000
3 Mo	-11.29	2.10	2.13	69 23	8,871
6 Mo	-8.98	4.17	3.83	65 14	9,102
1 Yr	-12.23	5.75	5.63	61 13	8,777
3 Yr Avg	-5.24	3.93	4.34	69 22	8,509
5 Yr Avg	4.78	1.12	1.32	48 20	12,630
10 Yr Avg	11.51	0.09	0.44	15 22	29,726
15 Yr Avg	11.00	0.14	0.37	14 24	47,846

Tax Analysis	Tax-Adj Rtn%	%Rank Cat	Tax-Cost Rat	%Rank Cat
3 Yr Avg	-6.04	17	—	—
5 Yr Avg	4.11	12	0.63	17
10 Yr Avg	10.82	8	0.61	4

Potential Capital Gain Exposure: 23% of assets

Rating and Risk

Time Period	Load-Adj Return %	Morningstar Rtn vs Cat	Morningstar Risk vs Cat	Morningstar Risk-Adj Rating
1 Yr	-12.23			
3 Yr	-5.24	+Avg	Low	★★★★
5 Yr	4.78	+Avg	-Avg	★★★★
10 Yr	11.51	+Avg	-Avg	★★★★
Incept	13.71	—		

Other Measures	Standard Index S&P 500	Best Fit Index S&P 500
Alpha	-0.2	-0.2
Beta	0.69	0.69
R-Squared	77	77
Standard Deviation	12.72	
Mean	-5.24	
Sharpe Ratio	-0.88	

Morningstar's Take by Brian Portnoy 03-27-02

The management team at Dreyfus Appreciation makes running a successful fund look so simple.

Chances are you're familiar with nearly every company in this fund's portfolio. Over several decades, Fayez Sarofim, who heads the team that subadvises the fund for Dreyfus, has built a stellar reputation and record by investing in brand-name global companies such as Coca-Cola, Johnson & Johnson, and General Electric. Most of this fund's holdings are equally prominent in their respective industries and are the same names that most of its large-cap competition owns as well.

Yet with the same names, the fund has earned above-par results year after year. Over the past 10 years, it has beaten 80% of its large-blend peers and has nipped at the heels of the S&P 500 index. And it has done so with much less volatility than average, thanks largely to its focus on market bellwethers and its measured approach to pricey growth issues from the tech, telecom, and media sectors.

An aversion to aggressive fare made for disappointing results in the frenzy of 1999, but that has translated into significant ballast during the ongoing market downturn. For example, in 2001, a year when the mega-caps that are this fund's specialty were among the market's worst performers, it still beat the market thanks to good showings from Johnson & Johnson and Philip Morris. Those same names, plus its energy and retail holdings, are spurring 2002's fine marks as well. For the year to date through March 26, its 2.5% gain ranks in the category's top 5%.

The fund's an excellent choice to anchor one's portfolio. Because management rarely tinkers with its holdings—its turnover ratio of 4% indicates that the fund has owned most of its stocks for years—it's also tax-efficient. Its expenses are reasonable, too.

Address:	144 Glenn Curtiss Blvd Uniondale, NY 11556-0144 800-373-9387
Web Address:	www.dreyfus.com/funds
Inception:	01-18-84
Advisor:	Dreyfus
Subadvisor:	Fayez Sarofim & Company
NTF Plans:	Fidelity Retail-NTF, Schwab OneSource

Minimum Purchase:	$2500	Add: $100	IRA: $750
Min Auto Inv Plan:	$100	Add: $100	
Sales Fees:	No-load		
Management Fee:	0.55% mx./0.27% mn.		
Actual Fees:	Mgt:0.55%	Dist: —	
Expense Projections:	3Yr:$284	5Yr:$493	10Yr:$1096
Income Distrib:	Annually		
Total Cost (relative to category):	Below Avg		

Portfolio Analysis 03-31-02

Share change since 12-01 Total Stocks:50	Sector	PE	YTD Ret%	% Assets
Pfizer	Health	27.1	-16.38	6.77
⊖ Johnson & Johnson	Health	27.1	-10.39	5.28
ExxonMobil	Energy	22.9	2.48	5.11
Philip Morris	Goods	10.5	4.29	4.58
Intel	Hardware	70.3	-42.82	4.27
Fannie Mae	Financial	13.1	-11.34	4.26
General Elec	Ind Mtrls	21.4	-28.63	3.84
Citigroup	Financial	13.1	-25.02	3.47
Walgreen	Consumer	40.2	11.62	3.30
Merck	Health	16.1	-21.26	2.98
PepsiCo	Goods	31.9	-6.48	2.96
Coca-Cola	Goods	46.7	20.64	2.87
Marsh & McLennan	Financial	26.9	-12.11	2.50
Wal-Mart Stores	Consumer	35.5	-4.80	2.49
BP PLC ADR	Energy	15.6	8.90	2.38
Microsoft	Software	48.0	-19.71	2.28
Procter & Gamble	Goods	40.0	12.76	2.16
McGraw-Hill	Media	30.3	-4.55	2.06
SBC Comms	Telecom	19.4	-20.17	2.02
Abbott Labs	Health	22.6	-35.97	1.99

Current Investment Style

Value Blend Growth — Large/Mid/Small

Market Cap %	
Giant	80.2
Large	18.8
Mid	1.0
Small	0.0
Micro	0.0

Median $mil: 106,544

Value Measures		Rel S&P 500
Price/Earnings	25.0	1.0
Price/Book	4.5	0.5
Price/Sales	1.6	0.8
Price/Cash Flow	10.0	0.8
Dividend Yield %	2.0	2.0

Growth Measures	%	Rel S&P 500
Projected Earnings	—	—
Book Value	12.0	0.9
Sales	12.0	1.3
Cash Flow	11.0	0.9
Trailing Earnings	11.0	0.9

Profitability	%	Rel S&P 500
Return on Equity	20.9	1.2
Return on Assets	11.3	1.4
Net Margin	9.9	1.1

Sector Weightings	% of Stocks	Rel S&P 500	3 Year High Low
Info	17.6	0.7	— —
Software	2.4	0.5	— —
Hardware	6.3	0.6	— —
Media	3.9	1.1	— —
Telecom	5.1	1.1	— —
Service	47.9	1.1	— —
Health	19.9	1.4	— —
Consumer	7.3	0.8	— —
Business	0.9	0.3	— —
Financial	19.7	1.1	— —
Mfg	34.5	1.1	— —
Goods	17.7	1.9	— —
Ind Mtrls	6.9	0.6	— —
Energy	9.9	1.4	— —
Utilities	0.0	0.0	— —

Composition

● Cash	3.4
● Stocks	94.7
● Bonds	0.0
○ Other	1.8
Foreign	4.7
(% of Stock)	

 MORNINGSTAR® Mutual Funds

NAIC®

Investment Education Since 1951

www.better-investing.org

STOCK FUND
Check List™

(A) Fund Name: _____

(B) Ticker Symbol: _____

(C) Category: _____

(D) Minimum Purchase($): _____ (E) Addt l($): _____

(F) Min Auto Inv Plan($): _____ (G) Addt l($): _____

(H) IRA($): _____

(I) Data Reference: _____ (J) Page No. _____

(K) Current NAV($): _____

(L) Total Assets($): _____

(M) Taxable: _____ (N) Tax-Deferred: _____

---

1. FUND INVESTMENT CHARACTERISTICS

A. Stated Investment Objective: _____

 • What are the fund s investment criteria & investment policies?

B. Portfolio Composition:

Cash	Stocks	Bonds	Other	Foreign
%	%	%	%	%

 • A cash holding of 20% or more may indicate the manager is trying to time the market...very risky!

C. Market Capitalization:

Giant	Large	Medium	Small	Micro
%	%	%	%	%

 • Are the assets concentrated according to the stated objective?

D. Total # of holdings: _____   E. Portfolio Analysis Date: _____

F. Top 10 Company Holdings:

No.	Company Name	Sector	Assets
1			%
2			%
3			%
4			%
5			%
6			%
7			%
8			%
9			%
10			%
			% Total

 • Does any one holding make up a far greater percent of assets than the others?

G. Portfolio Sector Analysis (%):

Info _____: Software _____ Hardware _____ Media _____ Telecom _____

Service _____: Health _____ Consumer _____ Business _____ Financial _____

Manufacturing _____: Goods _____ Ind Mtrls _____ Energy _____ Utilities _____

 • The fewer number of holdings and sectors that the fund s assets are spread over the greater likelihood for volatility within the portfolio.

five years or more, demonstrating a long-term commitment to the shareholders of that fund.

Make sure the fund manager's performance track record is strong, bettering a comparable market index. Indexes that you might want to compare a large growth fund to include the S&P 500, an index of 500 of the largest and most well known U.S. companies, and the Wilshire 5000, which follows the total stock market.

Pay close attention to fund costs. Every dollar you spend on fund fees is one less dollar you have to invest. Since most fund fees are deducted from your investment in the fund on a percentage basis, they can exert a silent drain on your account, especially if they are higher than average. Investors not only cover the operating expenses of a fund—known as the expense ratio—they also pay for brokerage costs when a fund manager buys and sells securities in the fund's portfolio.

After you gather all this information—which is easy to do, given the framework of the Check List—you'll know if a fund meets your investing requirements. If you've found several good funds, use the Comparison Guide to pick the best of the best. Once you've purchased shares in a fund, keep up with its progress on the Trend Report.

SUMMARY

The NAIC mutual fund program offers tools to help you find, compare and follow stock & bond mutual funds. These tools focus on a fund's key elements: its portfolio, management and costs. Use these tools to find a fund with a strong portfolio, experienced management and low costs.

KEY WORDS

PORTFOLIO
MANAGEMENT
COSTS
STOCK FUND CHECK LIST
**STOCK FUND
COMPARISON GUIDE**
**STOCK FUND TREND
REPORT**

QUESTIONS & ACTIVITIES

1. What key characteristics of a stock fund do the tools in the NAIC mutual fund program focus on?

    ▪

2. Which NAIC stock fund form would you use to compare funds with each other?

    ▪

3. Why is it important to find out a fund's minimum purchase requirement before evaluating it?

    ▪

4. Look at the Morningstar report for Dreyfus Appreciation on Page 64. Answer the following questions: How long has the manager been with the fund? What is its minimum purchase amount? What is the current expense ratio? How high is the current turnover rate? Do you recognize the names of any of the companies in the portfolio?

Plugging the Leaks

Chapter Goals—

After studying and reviewing this chapter, you will be able to:

• Describe how inflation, transaction costs and taxes can reduce the returns on your investments.

• Show the impact of these factors by calculating nominal and real total returns.

• List measures you can take as a stock and/or mutual fund investor to reduce transaction costs.

• List four types of tax-deferred retirement plans.

• Describe how tax-deferred retirement plans can benefit you as a lifelong investor.

Introduction

When you are working hard to make your money grow through carefully chosen investments, you want to retain as much of your returns as you can. This chapter discusses the three main factors that tend to erode your returns and describes measures you can take to protect your investments.

The Big Three

When we say that our salary is $25,000 or $40,000 a year, we mean total (gross) salary. Take-home pay, the amount we receive after taxes are deducted, is considerably less than that. And if our work involves certain expenses—commuting, parking, lunches, wardrobe, tools and supplies—our net income, what we actually have to live on, is reduced even further. From an economic perspective, the best job is not always the one with the biggest salary. It may be a job that actually pays less, but reduces our travel costs and allows us to live where housing and other expenses are lower.

A similar logic holds for investing. The actual return on your investments is what you get back after all your costs, losses and taxes have been deducted. There are three primary factors that tend to drain off investment income and investors have to do whatever they can to minimize them. These three investment leaks are (a) inflation, (b) fees and transaction costs, and (c) taxes.

Nominal & Real Total Returns

The following hypothetical example shows how to measure the impact of inflation, transaction costs and taxes on the one-year returns of a stock investment by calculating and comparing nominal and real total returns.

Mr. Johnson purchased 100 shares of stock for $2000 on March 1, 2002. The broker's fee (transaction cost) was $35. He held the stock for 12 months and a day and then sold it for $2400 (less another transaction cost of $35). He received $40 in cash dividends. His income taxes on this transaction were $55 (15% tax bracket). The inflation rate was 3%. What were Mr. Johnson's nominal and real total returns?

NOMINAL AND REAL TOTAL RETURNS
A HYPOTHETICAL EXAMPLE

NOMINAL TOTAL RETURNS	$2400	selling price	
	- 2000	buying price	
	= 400	capital gain	
	+ 40	dividend income	
	= 440	nominal total return	22% (440/2000)
REAL TOTAL RETURNS	2365	selling price	($2400 - $35 fee)
	- 2035	buying price	($2000 + $35 fee)
	= 330	capital gain	
	+ 40	dividend income	
	- 55	income tax	
	= 315	net return	16% (315/2000)
		- 3% inflation rate	
		13% real total return	

Inflation

Although inflation has been unusually low for the past several years in the United States, it remains a simple fact of life. You are as powerless to stop inflation as you are to keep the wind from blowing. What you must do instead is allow for inflation and choose investments with a good prospect of delivering returns that are considerably higher than historical inflation rates.

Fees & Transaction Costs

There are a number of measures you can take to reduce this drain on your investments. First of all, you can become more self-reliant. When you buy and sell stocks, you can do your own investment research and you can reduce brokerage fees by dealing with discount brokers. You can even make your stock transactions over the Internet, which is very inexpensive compared to dealing with a full-service broker.

If you are truly a long-term investor, you should not be engaged in constantly buying and selling stocks in response to changing stock prices. You should buy high-quality growth stocks in the first place and, with few exceptions, hang on to them for a long period of time. Every time you buy or sell a stock you incur transaction costs and these costs have a negative effect on real total returns.

Transaction costs can be zero with certain types of direct purchase plans and dividend reinvestment plans (DRIPs). Several hundred corporations, mostly large ones, provide opportunities to purchase their common stock directly from the corporation. Low cost plans are very similar, except for the fact that there is a nominal fee to purchase the first share, but no commission on subsequent shares. The NAIC offers a Low Cost Investment Plan with a very low one-time set-up fee.

The obvious way for mutual fund investors to reduce their fees and transaction costs is to do their own research and buy index funds or low-cost, no-load mutual funds. Mutual fund expense ratio information is readily available to mutual fund investors who do their homework. But there is also a second way for mutual fund investors to lower these costs. They can select funds with relatively low turnover rates in their stock portfolios. Overactive fund managers can really reduce the productivity of mutual fund investments.

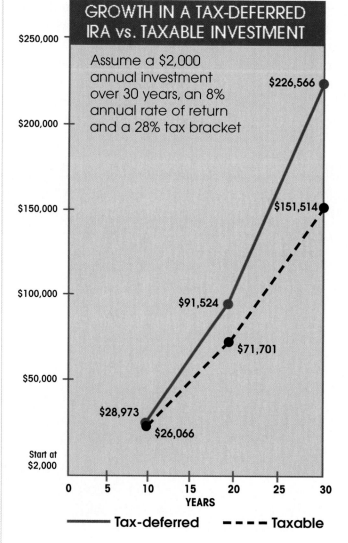

GROWTH IN A TAX-DEFERRED IRA vs. TAXABLE INVESTMENT

Assume a $2,000 annual investment over 30 years, an 8% annual rate of return and a 28% tax bracket

$250,000

$226,566

$200,000

$151,514

$150,000

$100,000

$91,524

$71,701

$50,000

$28,973

$26,066

Start at $2,000

0 5 10 15 20 25 30
YEARS

—— Tax-deferred   - - - - Taxable

Taxes

Investment income is subject to federal income taxes, as is any other income. Interest and dividends are taxable income and when you sell an investment for a higher price than you originally paid for it, you are subject to taxes on the capital gain.

As a young investor still in school and not working full time, taxes may not have much immediate effect on your investments, but you need to be aware of the fact that they will affect your ability to build up the value of your investments in the long run. Strange as it may seem, it is not too early to include tax-sheltering retirement plans in your investment strategy.

In order to encourage more Americans to engage in long-term investing and save for their retirement, the U.S. Congress has established a variety of tax deferring and tax-reducing retirement plans. Over the course of your life, these plans can make a huge difference in the amount of money you will be able to save.

401(k), IRA & Keogh Tax-Deferred Retirement Plans

These retirement plans allow people to defer taxes on their investments and their investment earnings until they begin withdrawing money from them. Tax-deferred retirement plans have two major advantages:
(a) The money you contribute to them is deducted from your income before your income taxes are assessed, thereby lowering the amount of your income that is subject to taxes.
(b) Since taxes on capital gains are also deferred until you take the money out, you will be able to accumulate a far larger sum of money before you begin making withdrawals.

401(k) Plans

—permit corporate employees to contribute a portion of their earned income up to a maximum limit to a tax-deferred account. Typically, the employee has a choice of funds to invest in—a growth stock fund, a balanced fund, a bond fund or a money market fund. Sometimes the employer contributes. Dividends, interest and capital

gains are not taxed until the person begins to make withdrawals (after age 59 1/2). There are expensive penalties for early withdrawal.

403(b) Plans

—are similar to 401(k)s, except for the fact that these plans are for employees of nonprofit organizations such as schools, hospitals, religious organizations and foundations.

457 Plans

—are available to state and local government employees.

Individual Retirement Accounts (IRAs)

—are for people who are not covered by an employer-sponsored retirement plan and for some who are covered, but do not exceed a specific income limit. An individual may establish an IRA and contribute up to a specified maximum amount each year (recently $3,000/year) plus a similar amount for a non-employed spouse.

SEP-IRAs & Keogh Plans

—are tax-deferred retirement plans for self-employed persons. They permit a larger maximum annual contribution than an IRA.

Roth IRA Retirement Plans

—Since 1998, the Roth IRA has offered another excellent tax-saving retirement option. Taxes are not deferred on Roth IRAs. Contributions are made with after-tax dollars and the initial investment is reduced by that amount. But taxes are not assessed on capital gains and no taxes are due when money is withdrawn (after age 59). The Roth IRA grows more slowly at first, but over the long haul produces more retirement income.

Arrangements

Employers generally handle 401(k), 403(b) and 457 Plans. Arrangements to place stocks or mutual funds in an IRA or Keogh Plan can be made through your broker or directly with a mutual fund company.

Life Insurance Contracts– Tax-Deferred

In addition to tax-deferred retirement plans, people may purchase annuity contracts and certain types of life insurance contracts with tax deferral features.

Information Source

The Internal Revenue Service (IRS) has published a "Student's Guide to Federal Income Taxes," IRS Publication 4—
www.irs.gov/pub/irs-pdf/p4.pdf

SUMMARY

Smart lifelong investors always try to (a) outperform inflation, (b) hold down investment costs and fees and without breaking any laws, (c) give as little of their growing wealth as possible to the taxman.

KEY WORDS

GROSS INCOME (SALARY)
TAKE-HOME PAY
NET INCOME
NOMINAL TOTAL RETURNS
REAL TOTAL RETURNS
CAPITAL GAINS
TAX-FREE
TAX DEFERRED
401(k) PLANS
403(b) PLANS
IRA
SEP-IRA
ROTH IRA
KEOGH PLAN
IRS

QUESTIONS & ACTIVITIES

1. Why does it sometimes make economic sense not to take the job with the biggest salary?

   ■

2. In the Real Total Returns calculations, (a) why is $35 added to the buying price and subtracted from the selling price? And where do the $315 and $2000 come from that are used to determine the net return percentage?

   ■

3. As an investor, what can you do about inflation?

   ■

4. Name two things you can do to save on transactions costs.

   ■

5. What do the different kinds of tax-deferred retirement plans have in common? How is each designed for a different group of workers?

   ■

6. How does a tax-deferred retirement plan save you money each time you contribute and over the entire life of the plan?

Protecting Yourself

Chapter Goals–

After studying and reviewing this chapter you will be able to:

- Explain what insurance is and how it works.
- Describe the major kinds of insurance people need.
- List the types of protection included in automobile insurance.
- Describe the main variables in medical insurance.

- Explain why and when people need life insurance.
- Compare the two main categories of life insurance.
- Describe the two kinds of property insurance.
- Indicate where you would go for ratings of insurance companies.

Introduction

At this stage of your life, you probably do not know a lot about insurance. Usually, insurance is something your parents buy, and you are covered by their policies. If you get sick and go to the hospital, their insurance covers the bill. If you have a driver's license, they pay more to insure the family car so that you are covered on the policy. As you become involved in investing, insurance will become more important to you. It is a key element in lifelong financial planning.

What Is Insurance & How Does It Work?

The basic idea behind insurance is simple. Insurance provides protection against financial losses. Often it helps you survive an event that could have resulted in financial disaster.

- Loss of income–as a result of illness, disability, death.
- Medical expenses–due to an accident or a health problem.
- Damaged property–from an accident, theft, natural disaster.
- Lawsuit–because you and/or your property were involved in an injury or loss to another person.

Insurance works by pooling the money of policyholders. Theoretically, any group of people with enough money could insure themselves. Each would contribute a sum of money to the insurance pool, which would compensate a group member who suffers an accident or a loss. Insurance companies take on the work

of forming pools, collecting payments from members and distributing funds when losses occur. Insurance companies also add to the pool of money by investing it. They add charges to pay themselves for providing these services.

The policyholder's contribution for insurance coverage (monthly, annual, single payment, etc.) is called a premium. The size of the premium is determined by (a) the potential size of the loss you are trying to cover and (b) the level of risk that this loss may occur.

Automobile Insurance

Automobile insurance protects you against losses due to (a) property damage, (b) personal injury and (c) injury to others. As you may already know, auto insurance for teen drivers is very expensive, and together with the other costs involved in owning and operating an automobile may eat up most of a teenager's money so that there is little or nothing left over for short-term or long-term investing.

You may not like all the options, but the best ways

of saving money on auto insurance include:

1. You decide not to own a car. Instead you rely on public transportation, a bicycle and occasional use of a family car.

2. You buy a car that is more than five years old and carry no collision or comprehensive coverage. In other words, you carry insurance for bodily injury and liability, but do not insure your own car.

3. You avoid high-powered sports cars that cost more to insure.

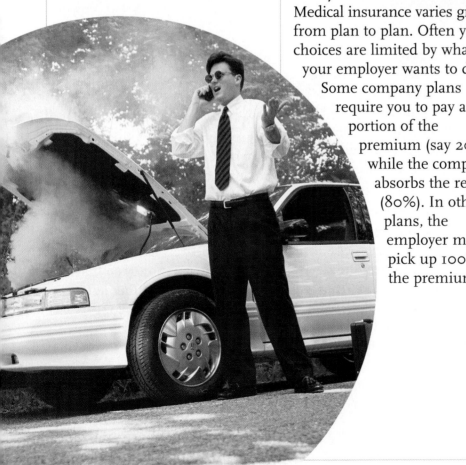

4. You insure your car, but with a $500 deductible. Your insurance reimburses you for damage to your car only after you have paid the first $500.

5. You do your best to maintain a flawless driving record. If you have an accident or a traffic violation, your insurance premiums will probably go up.

Medical Insurance

Although most people have medical insurance through their employers, more and more people are being required to buy their own insurance. Medical insurance varies greatly from plan to plan. Often your choices are limited by what your employer wants to do. Some company plans require you to pay a portion of the premium (say 20%) while the company absorbs the rest (80%). In other plans, the employer may pick up 100% of the premium.

Other common variables among medical insurance plans include:

Annual Deductible

—the amount you must pay on your medical bills each year before your insurance goes into effect.

Co-insurance (copay)

—the percentage of medical costs the insured person must pay (after paying the deductible). The share ratio is typically 20% by the insured person and 80% by the insurance company. At a specified stop-loss limit, $1000 or $2000 for example, the insurance company begins to pay 100% of the additional medical costs.

Maximum Coverage

—the lifetime limit on the total amount your insurance company will pay. Some HMOs (health maintenance organizations) have unlimited coverage because they can exercise greater control over costs than traditional policies.

Disability Insurance

Another type of health insurance is disability insurance. Many large employers provide disability insurance for their employees. Self-employed persons should consider purchasing their own. This type of insurance enables you to receive a certain portion of your salary when you are unable to work because of an accident or injury. Usually disability coverage is limited to one-half or two-thirds of gross salary. The limit is designed to give a worker an incentive to return to work as soon as possible.

Life Insurance

When you are older, hold a full-time job and begin to take on family responsibilities, you will need life insurance. The main object of life insurance is to provide financial protection to people who depend on you. The insurance will replace income that is lost as a result of your death. Generally speaking, you do not need life insurance before you have a family.

Before you buy life insurance, you should educate yourself about the different kinds of policies that are available. The many different types of life

insurance fall into two general categories:

Term Insurance

—the simplest and least expensive form of insurance, which allows you to buy coverage for a year or a specific period of time. If you die during that time, term insurance pays your beneficiary a sum of money.

Cash Value Insurance

—like term insurance pays a death benefit, but also builds up a cash value, which can be borrowed against or withdrawn when the policy is terminated.

You may want to buy term insurance when you are in your 20s and 30s and coverage is very inexpensive, and then stop buying life insurance when the value of your investments is large enough to protect your survivors. This is a cost-effective way of using insurance in conjunction with a lifelong investment program.

Those who do not have a long-term investment program may be interested in some form of cash value insurance, which will also serve as an enforced

savings program. Cash value insurance includes:

Whole life—premiums never change, offers death benefit, but also builds up a significant cash value over a period of time.

Variable whole life—allows you to choose how your insurance money is invested and decide how much risk you want to take on when trying to achieve a high level of return.

Universal life—allows you to vary your annual contributions.

Property Insurance

Property insurance includes real property insurance (a house or condominium) and personal property insurance (furniture, electronic equipment, jewelry. etc.) Property insurance will compensate you for a loss of property due to fire, theft, natural disaster and other hazards spelled out in your contract.

Your first living quarters outside your parents' house will probably be an apartment. You will not need real property insurance, but you may want renter's insurance to cover personal property. You should have a list of all your property in case you need to file a claim. It may also be useful to keep receipts for the more expensive items in a safe deposit box and to videotape these items on a periodic basis.

Liability Insurance

Liability insurance protects you from potential losses due to legal actions taken against you because of some alleged negligence. Liability coverage is included in auto and homeowner insurance. In a homeowner policy it covers lawsuits that may result from a person falling on your sidewalk or being bitten by your dog.

Buying Insurance

Before you buy insurance you need to compare policies to see how they stack up against one another. You should do business with an experienced agent who is designated as a chartered life underwriter, and before you buy, you should go to the Best Insurance Reports in your public library and make sure the company you are doing business with has an A rating or better from A.M. Best, an independent insurance rating company.

Information Sources on the Internet

The Internet contains a number of Web sites with insurance information. The Insurance Information Institute is found at *www.iii.org* and contains consumer information on a variety of insurance topics including homeowner, auto, and personal property.

Life Insurance Analysis Center—*www.underwriter.com*.

SUMMARY

Insuring your property, life and health will be critical to your financial well-being. You are learning how to build wealth over an extended period of time through investing. Appropriate insurance will protect you from losses that could wipe out your assets and undermine your investment program.

KEY WORDS

INSURANCE
PREMIUM
AUTOMOBILE INSURANCE
DEDUCTIBLE
MEDICAL INSURANCE
COPAY
MAXIMUM COVERAGE
DISABILITY INSURANCE
LIFE INSURANCE
TERM INSURANCE
CASH VALUE INSURANCE
LIABILITY INSURANCE
REAL PROPERTY INSURANCE
PERSONAL PROPERTY
   INSURANCE
A.M. BEST

QUESTIONS & ACTIVITIES

1.   In your own words describe how insurance works. How can an insurance company afford to pay someone $10,000 to repair an automobile damaged in an accident when the owner has contributed less than $1,000 in insurance premiums?

2.   Ask your parents to tell you about the insurance they have on their car(s). Do they have collision? Comprehensive? How much coverage do they have for injuries and property damage? How high is their deductible?

3.   You are sick for six months and cannot go to work. What type of insurance would cover a portion of your lost wages?

4.   Jerry has medical insurance with the following coverage: annual deductible of $200, 80/20 copay, stop-loss limit of $1,000 and a lifetime limit of $1 million. Jerry has a medical problem which totals $6,000 in one calendar year. How much will Jerry have to pay out of his own pocket?

5.   Julie is a college student and is single with no dependents. Would you advise her to buy life insurance? What would you tell her?

6.   Bill and Wendy are married, both employed, own a house and have a new daughter. Who should have life insurance in this household? Why?

7.   Discuss the differences between term life insurance and whole life insurance.

A Car and a House

Chapter Goals–

After studying and reviewing this chapter, you will be able to:

- List the steps you will take when you are ready to buy a car.
- Identify some written sources of information on buying cars.
- Name some Internet Web sites for used car buyers.
- Determine how much you can afford to pay for a car.
- Distinguish among the three basic types of home mortgages.
- Identify the advantages of home ownership vs. renting.
- Discuss the rules lenders use in determining what a prospective homebuyer can afford.

Introduction

In the not too distant future, you will probably face two major purchases: a car and a house. These are important decisions and they require a great deal of knowledge. This chapter will discuss the steps you should take when you are making these purchases and where to go for information. It will also help you weigh the impact of these "big ticket" items on your overall financial strategy.

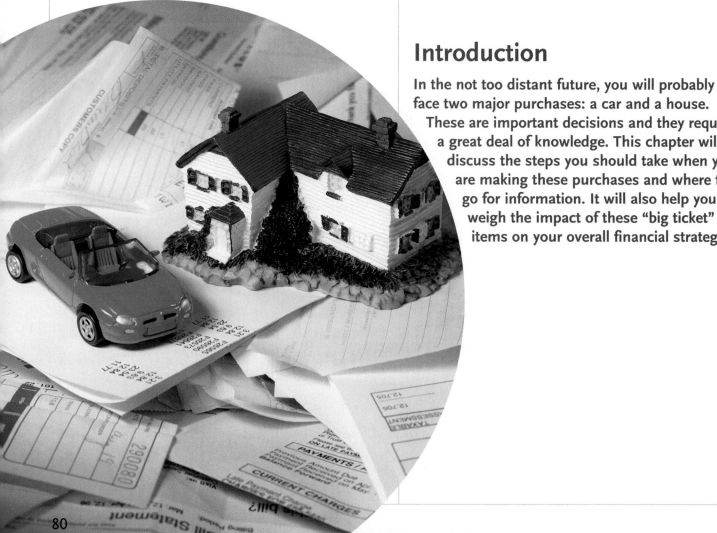

Contrasting the Two Purchases

Buying a car and buying a house have very different effects on your long-term finances. A car is a depreciating asset. It declines in value as it ages and most of the money you put into a car you will never get back. This suggests that you should put off buying a car until you absolutely need one and that you should not spend more on it than it takes to get a good, safe vehicle. A house, on the other hand, usually appreciates or increases in value through the years, and home ownership can make an important positive contribution to your long-term planning and investment strategy.

Buying a Car

Let's assume you have completed your education and are entering your chosen field of work. Your new employer pays a competitive salary and provides medical insurance, a 401(k) plan and life insurance. You need a car for commuting and you go through a step-by-step process like the one described in Chapter 1.

1. **Define your goal:** Buy a car that meets your needs.

2. **Collect Information:**

A. **Determine how much you can afford to spend.**

You prepare a monthly budget (see Chapter 3) to determine how much money you will have left over each month to spend on a car after you have covered your other regular expenses (rent, telephone, food, clothing, college loan, savings, incidentals, recreation). You calculate that you will need $200 a month for auto insurance and maintenance. Because you have invested wisely over the past seven years, you can withdraw $3,000 from your stock portfolio for a down payment. You shop around for the best auto loan rate you can find. You determine that you can comfortably handle monthly car payments of $206 a month—9% for 36 months on a total car loan of $6,000. You set a $9,000 limit on the car you will buy.

B. **Do research on used cars and buying them.**

Written Publications: There are thousands of books, articles and booklets on buying a car (new or used). Some contain checklists and pointers on how to make an intelligent car-buying decision. You should start with back issues of car and consumer magazines in the public library. *Consumer Reports* and *Changing Times* rate different models and rank them on safety, economy, performance and handling when new. These ratings will help you choose makes and models to look for. The *NADA Official Used Car Guide* has information on used car prices.

Internet Resources: One of the easiest ways to obtain automobile purchasing information on the Internet is to use Yahoo! (*www.yahoo.com*). Scan down to "Recreation and Sports" and then click on "Autos." There you can select "Buyer's Guides" and access all sorts of useful topics: used car checklists, used car databases, even a Web site on cars and trucks for tall people.

Particularly valuable are checklists of the items you should inspect (or have your mechanic inspect) before you buy. You can obtain used car prices from a number of Web sites, including

Edmund's Automobile Buyer's Guides, which contain a ton of good information *(www.edmunds.com)*. From the main home page, you can select "used cars" and read about topics such as:

- What You Should Know About the Used Car Industry
- How to Select the Used Car That's Right for You
- Where You Can Find a Great Used Car
- Pricing the Car
- Evaluating the Car
- How to Effectively Negotiate for a Used Car
- Closing the Deal on a Used Car
- How to Buy a Car from a Private Seller
- Quick 10-Step Guide to Buying Your Next Used Car
- One Final Suggestion: Take Your Time

This section also includes Edmund's ratings (by safety, reliability, performance, comfort, driving fun, value and overall), used car wholesale prices (what the dealer pays) and retail prices (what the dealer would charge you).

Note: For information on new cars, check out MSN Autos *(autos.msn.com)* and Kelley Blue Book *(www.kbb.com)*. MSN Autos is an information gold mine

that includes interactive videos of new cars, road test results, help on selecting a car based on your requirements and buying a car online. Kelley has new car summaries with dealer invoice prices and suggested retail prices.

3. **Explore your alternatives:** You visit the lots and check dealer advertisements and classified ads in your local newspaper. You talk to knowledgeable friends and relatives. You look at a number of cars in your price range and narrow the field down to a manageable handful of cars.

4. **Analyze the "pluses" and "minuses" of each alternative:** Using one of the checklists you have found, you should analyze the "pluses" and "minuses" for each of your finalists.

5. **Select the best alternative:** You choose the car you think makes the most sense for you and make an offer. You do a little "haggling" and settle on a price.

6. **Evaluate your experience:** From time to time, you review your experience and consider what you will do differently the next time you have to purchase a car.

Purchasing a House

If you are a teenager, buying a house is probably 10-to-15 years away and you may wonder—why worry about it now? But buying a house is one of the most important purchases and investments you will ever make. And it involves some real-life skills you will need to learn.

It is also important to realize that the investment skills you are learning can help you acquire money for the down payment. For example, if you save $10 a week and invest it in common stock or stock mutual funds on a monthly basis, at an annual return rate of 12%, your investment will be worth $21,648 at the end of 15 years. A total investment of $7,800 (780 weeks x $10) will grow to $21,648! If you invest $15 a week under the same conditions, in 15 years your investment will be worth $32,473! Over a period of time, small amounts of money invested regularly in common stocks or stock funds can grow into a "healthy" sum. An investment program can hold the key to home ownership, a wonderful addition to your quality of life—and your investment portfolio.

The Investment Advantage of Buying a House

When you rent a house or an apartment, each monthly payment is money "out the door." On the other hand, a mortgage payment on a house you are buying increases your equity (the amount you actually own).

A mortgage is a loan, from a bank or mortgage company, to someone buying real estate. A mortgage is "secured" by the property. If the borrower doesn't pay the mortgage payments in a timely manner, the lender can take the real estate to pay off the loan. At first, most of each month's mortgage payment is interest on the loan and only a little is applied to the debt (the principal). But over a period of time, as the debt goes down, more and more of the payment goes to reduce the principal.

As you pay off your mortgage, your equity in the property increases. But your equity can also increase in another way.

As the value of your property goes up, which property values normally do, your equity is growing. The house where you and your family are living is also an investment that is returning capital gains and increasing your wealth.

The Tax Advantages of Buying a House

The U.S. Tax Codes are designed to promote home ownership. And these tax benefits are another important advantage of owning a house over renting.

The interest you pay on your mortgage may be deducted from your gross income in determining your income tax. The property taxes on your home are also deductible and reduce your federal taxes. Because of these tax savings, people can afford to pay larger monthly mortgage payments than they can afford in rent. Home ownership has other tax advantages, too:

- As part of the Taxpayer Relief Act of 1997, Congress offered a provision that eliminates the federal income tax liability on the gain on the sale of a principal (primary) residence, for most people.

- Up to $250,000 of gain from the sale of a single person's principal residence is tax-free. For certain married couples, filing a joint tax return, the tax-free gain is $500,000.

Affording a House

How much house can you afford? A bank or mortgage company will look at the following factors:

- Current monthly income of the applicant.
- Expected future monthly income.
- The down payment.
- Current mortgage interest rates.
- The price of the house.
- Other debt obligations you may have.
- The number of years for the mortgage.

Generally, mortgage lenders look at gross monthly income in relation to the monthly housing payment, which includes the mortgage payment, property taxes and homeowner's insurance. The general rule of thumb states that the monthly housing payment should not exceed 30% of gross monthly income. Thus, a person earning $30,000 per year or $2,500 per month could afford a monthly housing payment of $750 ($2,500 x .30). Lenders also examine your other debts including auto loans and credit card debt. It is not unusual to hear of upper limits for all debt payments at 35% or 36% of gross income.

The Down Payment

The down payment is the amount of money you pay at the closing (the time of sale) from your own funds. The rest of the money for the house is loaned to you (the mortgage). If the down payment is less than 20% of the purchase price, the mortgage lender will normally require you to buy private mortgage insurance (PMI). This insurance protects the lender in case you default on the loan. Depending on the size of the mortgage, this additional insurance could cost several hundred dollars a year.

Knowing how much a lender will lend you and how much money you have for a down payment, you can figure out what you can afford to pay for a house. This amount is not hard to calculate and there are computer programs, especially on the Internet, which will walk you through. A real estate representative can also help.

Two Web sites with helpful general information for prospective home buyers (and sellers) are Home Buyer's Information Center *(www.ourfamilyplace. com/homebuyer/)* and the Prudential Real Estate Network *(www.prudential.com/realestate/)*.

Types of Mortgages

When you shop for a mortgage, you will find three basic types: fixed rate mortgages, adjustable rate mortgages (ARMs) and balloon mortgages.

Fixed Rate Mortgages

A fixed rate mortgage is just that, a mortgage with an interest rate that is fixed for the life of the mortgage and is not affected by changes in overall interest rates. The monthly payments never change and you always know how much to budget.

Adjustable Rate Mortgages

In contrast to a fixed rate mortgage, an adjustable rate mortgage, or ARM, has an interest rate that adjusts periodically (usually every three months) according to rising or falling interest rates in the overall economy. As a result, monthly housing payments may change on a quarterly basis, going up or down with overall interest rates. Usually, the initial rate on an ARM is lower than the rate on a fixed rate mortgage. ARMs may have a "cap limit" on the interest and a maximum change per year. Some ARMs allow you to convert to a fixed rate mortgage after a certain period of time.

Balloon Mortgages

The name comes from the fact that the borrower must pay off the mortgage in full at the end of the loan term. In other words, the payment at the end "balloons" to a sizable amount. Balloon mortgages are typically five or seven years in length. The interest rates on balloon mortgages are normally 3/8 to 3/4 of a percentage point below traditional fixed rate mortgages. Balloon mortgages are popular with homebuyers who expect to move before the end of the five-or-seven-year mortgage period. If you decide to stay in the house, you will have to pay the balance on the mortgage, or more likely, get another mortgage to pay off (refinance) the first mortgage.

Additional Information Sources for Home Buyers

Again, spending the time on research can save you big bucks. There are dozens of recent books for first-time homebuyers at your library or bookstore. The following paperback books should be available for less than $20:

Kiplinger's Buying & Selling a Home. By the staff of *Kiplinger's Personal Finance Magazine.* 1999. 374 pages.

Century 21 Guide to Buying Your First Home. Patrick Hogan and Century 21 editors. 1997. 208 pages.

Home Buying for Dummies.
Eric Tyson & Ray Brown. 2001.
384 pages.

*100 Questions Every First-Time
Home Buyer Should Ask.*
Ilyce R. Glink. Second Edition
2000. 510 pages.

*10 Steps to Home Ownership: A
Workbook for First-Time Buyers.*
Ilyce R. Glink. 1996. 351 pages.

Buy Your First Home. Robert
Irwin. Second Edition 2000.

*The 106 Common Mistakes
Homebuyers Make (And How to
Avoid Them).* Gary W. Eldred.
Second Edition 1998. 320 pages.

*The Unofficial Guide to Real
Estate Investing.* Spencer
Strauss & Martin J. Sone.
1999. Paperback, 446 pages.

SUMMARY

Buying a car and buying
a house are two of the
largest purchases you will
ever make. They require
special preparation and
study and you have to
consider them in your
overall financial plan.
This chapter has provided
an introduction to the
basic concepts and
concerns involved in these
"big ticket" purchases.

KEY WORDS

MORTGAGE
FIXED RATE MORTGAGE
ADJUSTABLE RATE
  MORTGAGE
BALLOON MORTGAGE
DEPRECIATE

APPRECIATE
DOWN PAYMENT
GROSS MONTHLY INCOME
MONTHLY HOUSING
  PAYMENT
RENT

QUESTIONS

1. How should the fact that a car is a depreciating asset affect your thinking about buying a car?

   ■

2. You are now 19 or 20 years of age and about to purchase your first car. Make a list of steps you will have to take to find out how much you can afford to spend.

   ■

3. With information available on the Internet, select one lower-priced (economy) new car, one medium-priced new car and one high-priced (luxury) new car. Compare the three alternatives. Explain which one you think is the best value.

   ■

4. A potential homebuyer with an annual gross income of $24,000 has approached a mortgage lender about receiving a mortgage on a house. How large a monthly housing payment would the typical lender say he could afford?

   ■

5. What is included in a "monthly housing payment?"

   ■

6. In addition to monthly car payments, what other car costs does a car owner face?

   ■

7. What are the major advantages of home ownership over renting?

   ■

8. Compare the three major types of home mortgages.

PART TWO:
Investing the NAIC Way

Writing Your Own Success Story

Chapter Goals–

After studying and reviewing this chapter, you will be able to:

- Explain NAIC's long-term investment philosophy.
- Summarize each of NAIC's four basic investment principles.
- Explain the logic of dollar cost averaging.

- Identify four regular, direct, low-cost methods of investing in stocks.
- Define the term "growth stock."
- Explain the concept of diversification.
- Compare the investment characteristics of large sales volume companies and small sales volume companies.

Introduction

In Part One you learned about the power of investing—what you can accomplish by contributing small sums of money on a regular basis to your investment portfolio. In Part Two you will learn the skills you need to pick stocks for your portfolio that will deliver an exciting rate of growth at a reasonable level of risk.

Your goal should be to double the value of your investments every five years. To do so will require an average 15% compounded annual gain in every five-year period. [Rule of 72: 72/15 = 4.8 years] You do not have to make 15% every year. Some years will probably return more than that, other years less. But following NAIC's basic investment principles, you should be able to achieve this goal.

Most of the information in Part Two is based on common stock selection methods developed many decades ago by the founders of NAIC. This information will provide the tools you need to manage your finances and control your destiny. After completing this course, your best financial advisor should be the person you see when you look in the mirror.

What Is the NAIC?

The National Association of Investors Corporation (NAIC) was founded in 1951 by four Michigan investment clubs that wanted to share information. The organization was set up to develop tools to assist long-term investors and to promote investment education. While originally established for investment clubs, the non-profit organization now provides investment education for both investment clubs and individual investors and has a total membership in excess of 300,000. Local NAIC Chapters, run by volunteers, provide investor workshops for their respective areas.

The NAIC Way of Investing

Through many years of experience, the NAIC has developed a long-term approach to investing which has proven very successful. This approach is founded on a fundamental analysis of companies, rather than just a technical analysis of stock performances (see Chapter 7). It revolves around NAIC's four basic investment principles. You have already encountered these principles, but we need to examine them in greater detail now:

1. Invest on a regular basis over a long period of time.

2. Reinvest all earnings (dividends, interest, capital gains).

3. Invest only in good quality companies with proven track records of growth.

4. Diversify your portfolio of companies to reduce overall risk.

NAIC'S Four Investment Principles

1. **Invest on a regular basis over a long period of time.**

Investing regularly over a long period of time has two important benefits. First, it provides a way for someone who does not have a lot of money to form an investment habit and begin building a portfolio. People who wait to begin investing until after they have made major purchases—car, house, furniture—will probably find themselves always trying to catch up with their debts and will certainly lose valuable time for their investments to grow and compound.

Regular investing also allows you to "dollar cost average." Dollar cost averaging means investing roughly equal amounts of money at regular intervals. Stock prices may move up or down, but when you spread your purchases out like this, you get more shares when the price is down. As a result, you will buy most of your shares at a price lower than the average price. Sounds tricky? See the example on the following page of how it works:

EXAMPLE OF DOLLAR COST AVERAGING:
YOU INVEST $25 A MONTH FOR A YEAR IN STOCK A.

First month stock price =	$15.00	Bought 1.666 shares
Second month price =	$15.50	Bought 1.612 shares
Third month price =	$16.00	Bought 1.562 shares
Fourth month price =	$16.50	Bought 1.515 shares
Fifth month price =	$17.00	Bought 1.470 shares
Sixth month price =	$17.50	Bought 1.428 shares
Seventh month price =	$18.00	Bought 1.388 shares
Eighth month price =	$18.50	Bought 1.351 shares
Ninth month price =	$19.00	Bought 1.315 shares
Tenth month price =	$19.50	Bought 1.282 shares
Eleventh month price =	$20.00	Bought 1.250 shares
Twelfth month price =	$20.50	Bought 1.219 shares
Average price =	$17.75	Total 17.058 shares

Total amount invested = $300 divided by 17.058 shares = average cost of $17.59 per share (vs. $17.75 average price per share).

The value of those 17.058 shares at the year-end price of $20.50 is $349.69. Since you paid $300 for them, you made $49.69, or a 16.56% gain in one year.

Low-cost ways of investing regularly include:

- NAIC's Low Cost Investment Plan.
- Buying direct from companies which provide that opportunity.
- Buying first shares from a broker and investing regularly in the dividend reinvestment plan (known as a DRIP plan).
- Joining an investment club or starting an investment club.

 Reinvest all earnings (dividends, interest & gains).

Reinvesting all earnings compounds your investment. It makes your earnings work for you as well as the money you originally invested. Reinvesting means:

- Reinvesting gains from the sale of stock
- Reinvesting dividends
- Reinvesting any interest earned.

Earnings should be reinvested in the stocks that produced the earnings (i.e. direct purchase or DRIP's) or in other common stocks. Remember, it is the power of compounding over a long period of time that produces superior performance. An investment that grows 10.41% per year will double in value every seven years. An investment that grows 14.87% annually will double every five years. An investment in short-term fixed income securities that produce a 5% annual total return will double in value in 14.87 years. That leads to the next basic principle.

 Invest in the common stock of good quality growth companies.

What is a growth stock or growth company? These are companies which are perceived to have excellent prospects for above-average future growth in revenues and earnings—and thus, in the price of their common stock. Growth companies are usually defined as companies that are growing faster than the rate of growth of the overall U.S. economy.

Quality growth companies should have established, continuous growth records for sales and earnings per share for at least five years and preferably longer (10 years).

Remember that continuous growth reflects strong management. You are interested in growth records because you are looking for companies which can provide consistent annual growth in net earnings over the next five years.

4. Diversify your investments.

By investing in different companies representing different industries, you reduce the risk of your overall portfolio. Investors call it diversification. An example of a poorly diversified portfolio: 15 companies, all in Internet-related businesses. A more diversified portfolio would contain stocks in several different industries.

In addition to diversifying by industry grouping, you can diversify by the size of companies you select based on: (1) sales volume and/or (2) market capitalization. Companies with sales over $5 billion are considered large, companies with sales between $500 million and $5 billion medium sized, and those with sales under $500 million small. Let's look at some of the attributes of large and small sales volume companies.

Advantages of a large sales volume company:

1. Business is more stable.
2. The stock price tends to be more stable.
3. The stock price should hold up better in a weak market.
4. Management should be able to control growth more efficiently through types of products sold.
5. The company may have a worldwide market.
6. Such companies should be purchased on dips in price.
7. Dividends may be larger as a percentage of earnings.

Disadvantages of a large sales volume company:

1. The growth rate in sales and earnings per share is normally less than 10%.
2. Sales have to increase by a much larger dollar amount to achieve the same percent of increase as a smaller company.
3. Dividends will be small if there is real potential for growth.

Advantages of a small sales volume company:

1. Sales and earnings growth rates can be higher than larger companies—we hope between 15-25%.
2. Yearly high and low prices will be farther apart due to greater price fluctuations.

Disadvantages of a small sales volume company:

1. Smaller companies are more likely than larger companies to experience falling stock prices in a weak market, especially when the country's economy is slow.
2. A smaller company may have more problems obtaining experienced and effective management.
3. Many smaller companies are family controlled and lack management depth.
4. Smaller companies are frequently younger and their survival rate is lower.

CHAPTER FOURTEEN

The Dot.com Crash and the Enron Scandal

In the 1990's, exciting increases in stock prices, especially Internet (dot.com) prices and other spectacular high flyers, tempted investors to abandon all four NAIC principles. People responded to rumors and hunches and threw their money at so-called buying opportunities. They invested in companies that were all promise, but had no track record. They did not worry about diversifying. For a while, some of them made impressive profits and looked very clever, but when the dot.com bubble burst and mighty Enron went bankrupt many of them lost nearly everything.

These highly publicized stock market catastrophes remind us that NAIC's four investment principles still make sense. Investors who remained faithful to them experienced relatively mild losses and, we believe, will not only survive them, but will go on to achieve the same kind of long-term gains in the stock market that patient, diversified investors who do their homework have always made.

Success Stories

NAIC has been helping investors for over fifty years. In those years, there have been many success stories. Many years ago, Tom O'Hara, former NAIC Chairman, told a young man that, if he saved $25 a month and invested it in good stocks, he could become a millionaire. The young man took the advice and invested $25 every month. Forty years later, at an NAIC conference, he showed Mr. O'Hara his stock portfolio. It had a total value of $1,300,000. "You were right," the man told Mr. O'Hara. Imagine what he will have if he continues to take advantage of the compounding effect of his investments and earnings and his portfolio doubles in value in the next five years!

Many of you will have great stories to tell, too. Stories of starting young, doing your homework and following NAIC's four basic principles.

SUMMARY

The NAIC lifelong investment philosophy can pay off for you. It will take patience and diligent work to do it. But your motivation will come from keeping your sights on the goal of doubling the value of your portfolio every five years and remembering how many five-year spans you have ahead of you to double and redouble your money.

Be patient in studying Part Two. Try to master the content of each chapter and each paragraph before moving on. Read other materials, tune in to radio and television programs, and talk with other investors to deepen your understanding of the terms and concepts you are learning. And follow NAIC's four basic investment principles.

Yes, it will take time, but when the gains start rolling in, you will be happy and proud you have used your time so wisely. You may have visions of helping with college expenses, starting your own business, having the down payment for your first home, or making a million dollars or more by the time you are 65 and ready to retire. You can accomplish them all.

KEY WORDS

COMPOUNDING
DIVERSIFY /
  DIVERSIFICATION
DIVIDENDS
DOLLAR COST AVERAGING
DRIP
FOUR INVESTMENT
  PRINCIPLES
GROWTH COMPANY
GROWTH STOCK
LOW COST INVESTMENT
  PLAN
NAIC
PORTFOLIO
REGULAR BASIS
REINVEST

PROJECTS

1. If you start now with $1,000 and double that amount through investing and compounding every five years, how many spans of five years will it take for you to become a millionaire? How old would you be?

   ■

2. Explain the importance of reinvesting all earnings in your portfolio.

   ■

3. Many investors in the late 1990's got caught up in the "technology bubble." Explain what can happen to a poorly diversified portfolio.

   ■

4. Memorize NAIC's four basic investment principles. Make sure you understand each of them.

   ■

5. Explain how dollar cost averaging enables you to buy stock at a below-average price.

   ■

6. Diversification increases the risk of a portfolio. (True or False)

   ■

7. Technical analysis is a major factor in the NAIC approach to choosing good long-term investments. (True or False)

Searching for Companies to Study

Chapter Goals—

After studying and reviewing this chapter, you will be able to:

- *Identify some methods for finding companies to study.*

- *Name the two independent sources of data on corporations you will use in completing the Stock Selection Guide.*

- *Describe the kinds of narrative and numerical information contained in Value Line and Standard & Poor's Stock Reports.*

- *Review a blank Stock Selection Guide and know where the initial data come from.*

- *Describe how you can obtain a company's annual report.*

Introduction

In Chapter 8, you were introduced to a host of investment information resources, everything from corporate publications to newsstand magazines and from radio and television programs to Internet Web sites. These sources will help you find stocks that arouse your interest. In this chapter, you will begin to examine the specific detailed information and information sources you will need to evaluate these investment prospects and choose the ones you want for your investment portfolio.

Where to Get Investment Ideas

1. **Take a look around you.**

One of the best ways to come up with investment ideas is simply to keep your eyes open and observe what is going on all around you. Is there a product or service you really love? Have you noticed a new restaurant chain which offers great food, at reasonable prices, with a fun atmosphere? Have you seen people using certain products or services that are growing in popularity? Are you aware of population or lifestyle trends that represent business opportunities? Are there problems that cry out for creative solutions—health problems, daily hassles, and service gaps? Almost every problem represents a business opportunity for somebody. Use your eyes and your ears. Sometimes a trip to the mall or a conversation with a friend can tell you a lot about investment opportunities.

2. **Read NAIC's *Better Investing* Magazine.**

This monthly magazine is a rich source for investment information and "stock to study" ideas. In the spring of each year, *BI* lists the names of the top 200 companies held by NAIC investment clubs. *Better Investing* can be obtained by subscription or through NAIC membership.

3. **Read other publications.**

As you know from reading Chapter 8, there are many excellent print and electronic sources of investment information. Let them stimulate your thinking. Learn what other investors are thinking. Use them to turn up more information on companies that interest you.

reading the descriptions of J&J on these pages and familiarizing yourself with the information they contain. See if you can find the items listed below on the appropriate sheets. They are numbered in the reports to help you find them. Don't worry about knowing what the terms mean. Definitions and explanations will be provided in the next few chapters.

Read the financial section of your local newspaper and consider companies in your own area. You will generally have an information edge on these companies compared with people in other parts of the country. If there are stocks that you are interested in buying or selling, watch their performance on the stock tables of your newspaper.

Check out the *Wall Street Journal* at your local library. It is the granddaddy of all business newspapers. Watch for information—hard numbers and written comments—on the companies that interest you.

4. Use Value Line and Standard & Poor's *Stock Reports.*

Two other sources of investment information recommended by the NAIC are Value Line and Standard & Poor's, which are found in most libraries. In Chapter 18 you will be introduced to the Stock Selection Guide (SSG), a four-page form that millions of investors have used to analyze stocks. Value Line and Standard & Poor's *Stock Reports* will provide the information you need to fill out the SSG and evaluate stocks for your portfolio.

Sample Value Line and Standard & Poor's *Stock Reports* on Johnson & Johnson are shown on the next few pages. You might be interested in

NOTE:

You will probably notice that Value Line assigns its data to the prior year and Standard & Poor's to the current year (the calendar year when the fiscal year ends). There are also some minor differences in the data because Value Line "normalizes" data by eliminating items that are unusual and do not recur year after year.

On the Standard & Poor's sheets find:

1. Total sales/revenues (different terms used in different industries)
2. Earnings per share
3. Quarterly sales
4. Quarterly earnings
5. Quarterly dividends
6. Yearly prices
7. Number of shares outstanding
8. Net before taxes
9. Book Value
10. P/E ratio
11. Beta
12. % retained on equity
13. % long term debt of capitalization
14. Institutional holdings
15. Dividends

On the Value Line page find:

1. Total sales/revenues
2. Earnings per share
3. Quarterly sales
4. Quarterly earnings
5. Quarterly dividends
6. Yearly prices
7. Number of shares outstanding
8. Tax rate
9. Net profit
10. Book value
11. Beta
12. % earned on net worth
13. Long term debt percent of capitalization
14. Insider holdings
15. Dividends

5. Utilize company information.

You can also find the above financial data in the annual reports of the companies you are researching. For beginners, however, the NAIC recommends using Value Line and Standard & Poor's because they summarize key information in easy-to-use formats.

You can usually get corporate information by calling the investor relations person at the company and asking for it. Both Value Line and Standard & Poor's provide company addresses and telephone numbers. Company annual reports are also available at many libraries and on the Internet.

STANDARD &POOR'S

STOCK REPORTS

Johnson & Johnson

NYSE Symbol **JNJ**

In S&P 500

28-JAN-03

Sub-Industry: Pharmaceuticals

Summary: The world's largest and most comprehensive health care company, JNJ offers a broad line of drugs, consumer products and other medical and dental items.

S&P Opinion: Accumulate (★★★★)

| Price As Of 1/24/03 • 53.61 | Yield • 1.5% |
| 52 Wk Range • 65.89-41.40 | 12-Mo. P/E • 24.6 |

Quantitative Evaluations

Outlook (1 Lowest—5 Highest)
• **2+**

Fair Value
• **45.70**

Risk
• **Low**

Earn./Div. Rank
• **A+**

Technical Eval.
• **Neutral** since 1/03

Rel. Strength Rank (1 Lowest—99 Highest)
• **37**

Insider Activity
• **NA**

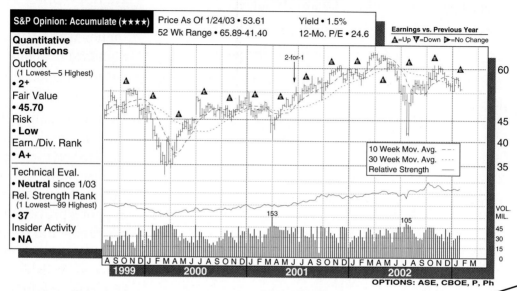

Earnings vs. Previous Year
△=Up ▽=Down ▷=No Change

10 Week Mov. Avg.
30 Week Mov. Avg.
Relative Strength

1999 2000 2001 2002

OPTIONS: ASE, CBOE, P, Ph

Overview - 20-DEC-02

We expect revenues to rise 11% in 2003. The gain should be led by a projected 70% increase in sales at the Cordis division, driven largely by the new Cypher drug-coated coronary stent. Introduced in Europe in April 2002, Cypher is expected to receive FDA approval in the spring of 2003. Strong gains are also seen for glucose monitoring products. Drug sales should benefit from continued growth in Procrit treatment for anemia, Duragesic transdermal patch for chronic pain, and Remicade anti-inflammatory agent. Consumer products sales should be modestly higher. Margins should benefit from an improved sales mix, productivity enhancements and higher other income. EPS in 2003 is projected at $2.62, up from $2.26 (before special charges) estimated for 2002.

Valuation - 20-DEC-02

The shares were highly volatile in recent months, mirroring turbulence in large capitalization medical stocks and several company specific developments. The stock sold off sharply in mid-July on news of a federal criminal investigation of a Puerto Rican plant, but bounced back as the case was subsequently dropped. More recently, JNJ was under pressure from safety issues and new competition in the Procrit/Eprex anti-anemia line, and concern over possible delays in FDA approval of the Cypher drug-coated coronary stent. However, we expect continued growth in market leader Procrit/Eprex, and we remain confident that Cypher will win FDA clearance in February or March 2003. With demonstrated high efficacy in preventing arterial reclogging after angioplasty, Cypher should generate sales of $1.7 billion in 2003. The stock, valued at a modest premium relative to other leading drug/medical companies, merits accumulation.

Key Stock Statistics

S&P EPS Est. 2003	2.62	Tang. Bk. Value/Share	4.32
P/E on S&P Est. 2003	20.5	Beta	0.44
Dividend Rate/Share	0.82	Shareholders	164,200
Shs. outstg. (M)	2970.6	Market cap. (B)	$155.0
Avg. daily vol. (M)	6.942	Inst. holdings	62%

Value of $10,000 invested 5 years ago: $ 17,113

Fiscal Year Ending Dec. 31

	2002	2001	2000	1999	1998	1997
Revenues (Million $)						
1Q	8,743	7,791	7,319	6,638	5,783	5,715
2Q	9,073	8,342	7,508	6,854	5,783	5,698
3Q	9,079	8,238	7,204	6,749	5,724	5,586
4Q	9,403	8,403	7,108	6,877	6,367	5,630
Yr.	36,298	33,004	29,139	27,471	23,657	22,629
Earnings Per Share ($)						
1Q	0.59	0.53	0.47	0.41	0.36	0.33
2Q	0.54	0.48	0.47	0.42	0.37	0.34
3Q	0.57	0.49	0.45	0.40	0.35	0.32
4Q	0.48	0.36	0.32	0.27	0.03	0.23
Yr.	2.18	1.84	1.70	1.47	1.11	1.21

Next earnings report expected: mid April

Dividend Data (Dividends have been paid since 1944.)

Amount ($)	Date Decl.	Ex-Div. Date	Stock of Record	Payment Date
0.205	Apr. 25	May. 17	May. 21	Jun. 11 '02
0.205	Jul. 15	Aug. 16	Aug. 20	Sep. 10 '02
0.205	Oct. 17	Nov. 15	Nov. 19	Dec. 10 '02
0.205	Jan. 06	Feb. 13	Feb. 18	Mar. 11 '03

For important regulatory information, go to www.standardandpoors.com, "Regulatory Disclosures"

A Division of The **McGraw·Hill** Companies

Reprinted with permission of Standard & Poor's, a division of the McGraw-Hill Companies

STANDARD &POOR'S

Johnson & Johnson

STOCK REPORTS

28-JAN-03

Business Summary - 20-DEC-02

Well known for household names like Tylenol and Band-Aid adhesive bandages, Johnson & Johnson ranks as the world's largest and most diversified health care company. JNJ traces its roots to James Johnson and Edward Mead Johnson, who formed the company more than 110 years ago. Today, JNJ offers an impressive list of blockbuster prescription drugs, medical instruments, and the broadest line of health-related consumer products.

Pharmaceuticals accounted for 45% of sales and 62% of operating profits in 2001; medical devices and diagnostics for 34% and 25%; and consumer products for 21% and 13%. JNJ is one of the most geographically diversified health care companies, with operations outside of the U.S. accounting for 39% of 2001 sales.

Despite its immense size, JNJ continues to generate robust earnings growth. While helped by an expanding health care marketplace, its outstanding success also reflects proficient management, which directed the company's growth through well planned, strategic acquisitions, aggressive R&D spending, and a policy of decentralized management. Over the past 10 years, JNJ acquired over 40 businesses, many of which have become important sources of growth. R&D spending totaled $3.6 billion in 2001, equal to 10.9% of sales.

Some of the more noteworthy fast-growing product lines developed or acquired in recent years include Remicade anti-inflammatory, Risperdal anti-psychotic, and Procrit anti-anemia drugs; the LifeScan home glucose monitoring system; and the Cypher drug-coated and BX Velocity coronary stents, used after angioplasty procedures. These and similar products enabled JNJ to post compound EPS growth (excluding nonrecurring items) of about 13% in the 10 years through 2001.

More than 90 different prescription drug, contraceptive and veterinary products are sold, with many generating sales in the hundreds of millions of dollars. The pharmaceutical division was enlarged in recent years through the acquisitions of ALZA, a leading drug delivery firm, and Centocor, a leading biotechnology company.

JNJ also holds leading positions in growing medical device and diagnostics lines. These include older items such as sutures, wound closure products, surgical accessories and orthopedic products, as well as newer products such as coronary stents, angioplasty catheters, and disposable contact lenses. The orthopedic business was significantly enlarged in 1998 with the purchase of DePuy. Although slower growing, consumer products such as Tylenol, bandages and toiletries provide a solid base of stability and cash flow.

Per Share Data ($)

(Year Ended Dec. 31)	2002	2001	2000	1999	1998	1997	1996	1995	1994	1993
Tangible Bk. Val.	NA	4.97	4.15	3.11	2.38	3.38	2.90	2.35	1.84	1.81
Cash Flow	NA	2.35	2.23	1.98	1.57	1.59	1.47	1.26	1.06	0.92
Earnings	2.18	1.84	1.70	1.47	1.11	1.24	1.08	0.93	0.78	0.69
S&P Core Earnings	NA	1.69	NA	NA	NA	NA	NA	NA	NA	NA
Dividends	0.80	0.70	0.62	0.55	0.49	0.43	0.37	0.32	0.28	0.25
Payout Ratio	36%	38%	36%	37%	43%	35%	34%	34%	36%	37%
Prices - High	65.89	60.97	52.96	53.43	44.87	33.65	27.00	23.09	14.12	12.59
- Low	41.40	40.25	33.06	38.50	31.68	24.31	20.78	13.40	9.00	8.90
P/E Ratio - High	30	33	31	36	40	27	25	25	18	18
- Low	19	22	19	26	28	20	19	14	12	13

Income Statement Analysis (Million $)

	2002	2001	2000	1999	1998	1997	1996	1995	1994	1993
Revs.	NA	33,004	29,139	27,471	23,657	22,629	21,620	18,842	15,734	14,138
Oper. Inc.	NA	9,490	7,992	7,370	6,291	5,689	5,312	6,002	3,531	3,011
Depr.	NA	1,605	1,515	1,444	1,246	1,067	1,009	857	724	617
Int. Exp.	NA	153	146	197	110	120	180	213	186	174
Pretax Inc.	NA	7,898	6,622	5,753	4,269	4,576	4,033	3,317	2,681	2,332
Eff. Tax Rate	NA	28.2%	27.5%	27.6%	28.3%	27.8%	28.4%	27.6%	25.2%	23.4%
Net Inc.	NA	5,668	4,800	4,167	3,059	3,303	2,887	2,403	2,006	1,787
S&P Core Earnings	NA	5,090	NA	NA	NA	NA	NA	NA	NA	NA

Balance Sheet & Other Fin. Data (Million $)

	2002	2001	2000	1999	1998	1997	1996	1995	1994	1993
Cash	NA	8,941	6,013	4,320	2,994	2,753	2,136	1,364	704	476
Curr. Assets	NA	18,473	15,450	13,200	11,132	10,563	9,370	7,938	6,680	5,217
Total Assets	NA	38,488	31,321	29,163	26,211	21,453	20,010	17,873	15,668	12,242
Curr. Liab.	NA	8,044	7,140	7,454	8,162	5,283	5,184	4,388	4,266	3,212
LT Debt	NA	2,217	2,037	2,450	1,269	1,126	1,410	2,107	2,199	1,493
Common Equity	NA	24,233	18,808	16,213	13,590	12,359	10,836	9,045	7,122	5,568
Total Cap.	NA	26,943	21,100	18,950	15,437	13,660	12,416	11,308	9,451	7,183
Cap. Exp.	NA	1,731	1,646	1,728	1,460	1,391	1,373	1,256	937	975
Cash Flow	NA	7,273	6,315	5,611	4,305	4,370	3,896	3,260	2,730	2,404
Curr. Ratio	NA	2.3	2.2	1.8	1.4	2.0	1.8	1.8	1.6	1.6
% LT Debt of Cap.	NA	8.2	9.7	12.9	8.2	8.2	11.4	18.6	23.3	20.8
% Net Inc.of Revs.	NA	17.2	16.5	15.2	12.9	14.6	15.3	12.8	12.7	12.6
% Ret. on Assets	NA	15.6	15.9	14.8	12.8	15.9	15.2	14.3	14.4	15.0
% Ret. on Equity	NA	25.4	27.4	27.5	23.6	28.5	29.0	29.7	31.6	33.6

Data as orig reptd.; bef. results of disc opers/spec. items. Per share data adj. for stk. divs. Bold denotes diluted EPS (FASB 128)-prior periods restated. E-Estimated. NA-Not Available. NM-Not Meaningful. NR-Not Ranked.

Office—One Johnson & Johnson Plaza, New Brunswick, NJ 08933. **Tel**—(732) 524-0400. **Website**—http://www.jnj.com **Chrmn & CEO**—W. C. Weldon. **Sr Vice Chrmn**—R. N. Wilson. **Vice Chrmn**—J. T. Lenehan. **EVP-Fin & CFO**—R. J. Darretta. **Secy**—M. H. Ullmann. **Treas**—J. A. Papa. **Investor Contact**—Helen E. Short (800-950-5089). **Dirs**—G. N. Burrow, J. G. Cullen, R. J. Darretta, M. J. Folkman, A. D. Jordan, A. G. Langbo, J. T. Lenehan, L. F. Mullin, H. B. Schacht, M. F. Singer, J. W. Snow, W. C. Weldon, R. N. Wilson. **Transfer Agent & Registrar**—EquiServe Trust Co., Jersey City, NJ. **Incorporated**—in New Jersey in 1887. **Empl**— 101,800. **S&P Analyst:** H. B. Saftlas/CB

Reprinted with permission of Standard & Poor's, a division of the McGraw-Hill Companies

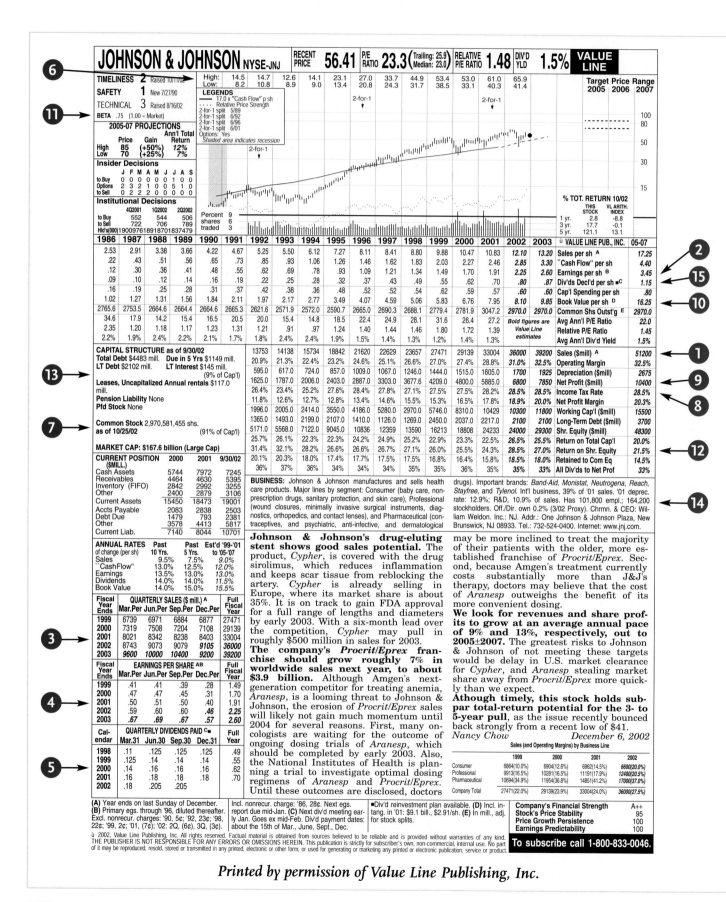

JOHNSON & JOHNSON NYSE-JNJ

| RECENT PRICE | 56.41 | P/E RATIO | 23.3 (Trailing: 25.9 / Median: 23.0) | RELATIVE P/E RATIO | 1.48 | DIV'D YLD | 1.5% | VALUE LINE |

TIMELINESS 2 Raised 10/11/02
SAFETY 1 New 7/27/90
TECHNICAL 3 Raised 8/16/02
BETA .75 (1.00 = Market)

| High: | 14.5 | 14.7 | 12.6 | 23.1 | 14.1 | 27.0 | 27.5 | 44.9 | 53.4 | 53.0 | 61.0 | 65.9 |
| Low: | 8.2 | 10.8 | 8.9 | 9.0 | 13.4 | 20.8 | 24.3 | 31.7 | 38.5 | 33.1 | 40.3 | 41.4 |

LEGENDS
— 17.0 x "Cash Flow" p sh
.... Relative Price Strength
2-for-1 split 5/89
2-for-1 split 6/92
2-for-1 split 6/96
2-for-1 split 6/01
Options: Yes
Shaded area indicates recession

Target Price Range
2005 2006 2007

2005-07 PROJECTIONS
	Price	Gain	Ann'l Total Return
High	85	(+50%)	12%
Low	70	(+25%)	7%

Insider Decisions
	J	F	M	A	M	J	J	A	S
to Buy	0	0	0	0	0	0	1	0	0
Options	2	3	2	1	0	5	1	0	0
to Sell	0	2	2	2	0	0	0	0	0

Institutional Decisions
	4Q2001	1Q2002	2Q2002
to Buy	552	544	506
to Sell	722	706	789
Hld's(000)	1900976	1891870	1837479

Percent shares traded 9 / 6 / 3

% TOT. RETURN 10/02
	THIS STOCK	VL ARITH. INDEX
1 yr.	2.8	-8.8
3 yr.	17.7	-0.1
5 yr.	121.1	13.1

	1986	1987	1988	1989	1990	1991	1992	1993	1994	1995	1996	1997	1998	1999	2000	2001	2002	2003	© VALUE LINE PUB., INC.	05-07
Sales per sh A	2.53	2.91	3.38	3.66	4.22	4.67	5.25	5.50	6.12	7.27	8.11	8.41	8.80	9.88	10.47	10.83	12.10	13.20		17.25
"Cash Flow" per sh	.22	.43	.51	.56	.65	.73	.85	.93	1.06	1.26	1.46	1.62	1.83	2.03	2.27	2.46	2.85	3.30		4.40
Earnings per sh B	.12	.30	.36	.41	.48	.55	.62	.69	.78	.93	1.09	1.21	1.34	1.49	1.70	1.91	2.25	2.60		3.45
Div'ds Decl'd per sh ■C	.09	.10	.12	.14	.16	.19	.22	.25	.28	.32	.37	.43	.49	.55	.62	.70	.80	.87		1.15
Cap'l Spending per sh	.16	.19	.25	.28	.31	.37	.42	.38	.36	.48	.52	.52	.54	.62	.59	.57	.60	.60		.80
Book Value per sh D	1.02	1.27	1.31	1.56	1.84	2.11	1.97	2.17	2.77	3.49	4.07	4.59	5.06	5.83	6.76	7.95	8.10	9.85		16.25
Common Shs Outst'g E	2765.6	2753.5	2664.6	2664.4	2664.6	2665.3	2621.6	2571.9	2572.0	2590.7	2665.0	2690.3	2688.1	2779.4	2781.9	3047.2	2970.0	2970.0		2970.0
Avg Ann'l P/E Ratio	34.6	17.9	14.2	15.4	16.5	20.5	20.0	15.4	14.8	18.5	22.4	24.9	28.1	31.6	26.4	27.2	Bold figures are Value Line estimates			22.0
Relative P/E Ratio	2.35	1.20	1.18	1.17	1.22	1.31	1.21	.91	.97	1.24	1.40	1.44	1.46	1.80	1.72	1.39				1.45
Avg Ann'l Div'd Yield	2.2%	1.9%	2.4%	2.2%	2.1%	1.7%	1.8%	2.4%	2.4%	1.9%	1.5%	1.4%	1.3%	1.2%	1.4%	1.3%				1.5%

CAPITAL STRUCTURE as of 9/30/02
Total Debt $4483 mill. Due in 5 Yrs $1149 mill.
LT Debt $2102 mill. LT Interest $145 mill.
(9% of Cap'l)
Leases, Uncapitalized Annual rentals $117.0 mill.
Pension Liability None
Pfd Stock None
Common Stock 2,970,581,455 shs. as of 10/25/02 (91% of Cap'l)
MARKET CAP: $167.6 billion (Large Cap)

	1986-2001 (see columns)																	
Sales ($mill) A						13753	14138	15734	18842	21620	22629	23657	27471	29139	33004	36000	39200	51200
Operating Margin						20.9%	21.3%	22.4%	23.2%	24.6%	25.1%	26.6%	27.0%	27.4%	28.8%	31.0%	32.5%	32.5%
Depreciation ($mill)						595.0	617.0	724.0	857.0	1009.0	1067.0	1246.0	1444.0	1515.0	1605.0	1700	1925	2675
Net Profit ($mill)						1625.0	1787.0	2006.0	2403.0	2887.0	3303.0	3677.6	4209.0	4800.0	5885.0	6800	7850	10400
Income Tax Rate						26.4%	23.4%	25.2%	27.6%	28.4%	27.8%	27.1%	27.5%	27.5%	28.2%	28.5%	28.5%	28.5%
Net Profit Margin						11.8%	12.6%	12.7%	12.8%	13.4%	14.6%	15.5%	15.3%	16.5%	17.8%	18.9%	20.0%	20.3%
Working Cap'l ($mill)						1996.0	2005.0	2414.0	3550.0	4186.0	5280.0	2970.0	5746.0	8310.0	10429	10300	11800	15500
Long-Term Debt ($mill)						1365.0	1493.0	2199.0	2107.0	1410.0	1126.0	1269.0	2450.0	2037.0	2217.0	2100	2100	3700
Shr. Equity ($mill)						5171.0	5568.0	7122.0	9045.0	10836	12359	13590	16213	18808	24233	24000	29300	48300
Return on Total Cap'l						25.7%	26.1%	22.3%	22.3%	24.2%	24.9%	25.2%	22.9%	23.3%	22.5%	26.5%	25.5%	20.0%
Return on Shr. Equity						31.4%	32.1%	28.2%	26.6%	26.6%	26.7%	27.1%	26.0%	25.5%	24.3%	28.5%	27.0%	21.5%
Retained to Com Eq						20.1%	20.3%	18.0%	17.4%	17.7%	17.5%	17.5%	16.8%	16.4%	15.8%	18.5%	18.0%	14.5%
All Div'ds to Net Prof						36%	37%	36%	34%	34%	34%	35%	35%	36%	35%	35%	33%	33%

CURRENT POSITION ($MILL.)
	2000	2001	9/30/02
Cash Assets	5744	7972	7245
Receivables	4464	4630	5395
Inventory (FIFO)	2842	2992	3255
Other	2400	2879	3106
Current Assets	15450	18473	19001
Accts Payable	2083	2838	2503
Debt Due	1479	793	2381
Other	3578	4413	5817
Current Liab.	7140	8044	10701

ANNUAL RATES
of change (per sh)	Past 10 Yrs.	Past 5 Yrs.	Est'd '99-'01 to '05-'07
Sales	9.5%	7.5%	9.0%
"Cash Flow"	13.0%	12.5%	12.0%
Earnings	13.5%	13.0%	13.0%
Dividends	14.0%	14.0%	11.5%
Book Value	14.0%	15.0%	15.5%

Fiscal Year Ends	QUARTERLY SALES ($ mill.) A Mar.Per	Jun.Per	Sep.Per	Dec.Per	Full Fiscal Year
1999	6739	6971	6884	6877	27471
2000	7319	7508	7204	7108	29139
2001	8021	8342	8238	8403	33004
2002	8743	9073	9079	9105	36000
2003	9600	10000	10400	9200	39200

Fiscal Year Ends	EARNINGS PER SHARE AB Mar.Per	Jun.Per	Sep.Per	Dec.Per	Full Fiscal Year
1999	.41	.41	.39	.28	1.49
2000	.47	.47	.45	.31	1.70
2001	.50	.51	.50	.40	1.91
2002	.59	.60	.60	.46	2.25
2003	.67	.69	.67	.57	2.60

Cal-endar	QUARTERLY DIVIDENDS PAID C■ Mar.31	Jun.30	Sep.30	Dec.31	Full Year
1998	.11	.125	.125	.125	.49
1999	.125	.14	.14	.14	.55
2000	.14	.16	.16	.16	.62
2001	.16	.18	.18	.18	.70
2002	.18	.205	.205		

BUSINESS: Johnson & Johnson manufactures and sells health care products. Major lines by segment: Consumer (baby care, non-prescription drugs, sanitary protection, and skin care), Professional (wound closures, minimally invasive surgical instruments, diagnostics, orthopedics, and contact lenses), and Pharmaceutical (contraceptives, and psychiatric, anti-infective, and dermatological drugs). Important brands: Band-Aid, Monistat, Neutrogena, Reach, Stayfree, and Tylenol. Int'l business, 39% of '01 sales. '01 deprec. rate: 12.9%; R&D 10.9% of sales. Has 101,800 empl.; 164,200 stockholders. Off./Dir. own 0.2% (3/02 Proxy). Chrmn. & CEO: William Weldon. Inc.: NJ. Addr.: One Johnson & Johnson Plaza, New Brunswick, NJ 08933. Tel.: 732-524-0400. Internet: www.jnj.com.

Johnson & Johnson's drug-eluting stent shows good sales potential. The product, *Cypher*, is covered with the drug sirolimus, which reduces inflammation and keeps scar tissue from reblocking the artery. *Cypher* is already selling in Europe, where its market share is about 35%. It is on track to gain FDA approval for a full range of lengths and diameters by early 2003. With a six-month lead over the competition, *Cypher* may pull in roughly $500 million in sales for 2003.

The company's *Procrit/Eprex* franchise should grow roughly 7% in worldwide sales next year, to about $3.9 billion. Although Amgen's next-generation competitor for treating anemia, *Aranesp*, is a looming threat to Johnson & Johnson, the erosion of *Procrit/Eprex* sales will likely not gain much momentum until 2004 for several reasons. First, many oncologists are waiting for the outcome of ongoing dosing trials of *Aranesp*, which should be completed by early 2003. Also, the National Institutes of Health is planning a trial to investigate optimal dosing regimens of *Aranesp* and *Procrit/Eprex*. Until these outcomes are disclosed, doctors may be more inclined to treat the majority of their patients with the older, more established franchise of *Procrit/Eprex*. Second, because Amgen's treatment currently costs substantially more than J&J's therapy, doctors may believe that the cost of *Aranesp* outweighs the benefit of its more convenient dosing.

We look for revenues and share profits to grow at an average annual pace of 9% and 13%, respectively, out to 2005±2007. The greatest risks to Johnson & Johnson of not meeting these targets would be delay in U.S. market clearance for *Cypher*, and *Aranesp* stealing market share away from *Procrit/Eprex* more quickly than we expect.

Although timely, this stock holds sub-par total-return potential for the 3- to 5-year pull, as the issue recently bounced back strongly from a recent low of $41.
Nancy Chow   December 6, 2002

Sales (and Operating Margins) by Business Line
	1999	2000	2001	2002
Consumer	6864(10.0%)	6904(12.6%)	6962(14.5%)	6600(20.0%)
Professional	9913(16.5%)	10281(16.5%)	11191(17.9%)	12400(20.5%)
Pharmaceutical	10694(34.9%)	11954(36.8%)	14851(41.2%)	17000(37.0%)
Company Total	27471(22.0%)	29139(23.9%)	33004(24.0%)	36000(27.5%)

(A) Year ends on last Sunday of December. (B) Primary egs. through '96, diluted thereafter. Excl. nonrecur. charges: '90, 5¢; '92, 23¢; '98, 22¢; '99, 2¢; '01, (7¢); '02: 2Q, (6¢), 3Q, (3¢). Incl. nonrecur. charge: '86, 28¢. Next egs. report due mid-Jan. (C) Next div'd meeting early Jan. Goes ex mid-Feb. Div'd payment dates: about the 15th of Mar., June, Sept., Dec. ■Div'd reinvestment plan available. (D) Incl. intang. in '01: $9.1 bill., $2.91/sh. (E) In mill., adj. for stock splits.

Company's Financial Strength A++
Stock's Price Stability 95
Price Growth Persistence 100
Earnings Predictability 100

To subscribe call 1-800-833-0046.

Printed by permission of Value Line Publishing, Inc.

SUMMARY

In order to choose the stocks that are right for you and to manage your investments wisely, you need good information on the companies you are investing in. The NAIC recommends getting that information from Value Line, Standard & Poor's, corporate annual and quarterly reports, and business journals and magazines.

KEY WORDS

BETTER INVESTING
STANDARD & POOR'S
STOCK SELECTION GUIDE
VALUE LINE

QUESTIONS & ACTIVITIES

1. Call or write a corporation and ask for the last two annual reports and any subsequent quarterly reports.

    ■

2. Take a look around your hometown or your state for companies you might want to study. Compile a list.

    ■

3. List some of the key data found in Value Line that are used in filling out the SSG.

    ■

4. Take your list of hometown or state companies (question #2) to the library and see how many you can find in Value Line or S&P.

    ■

5. What are some of the major trends (lifestyles, recreation, technology, demographics) that are visible in the United States right now? Identify companies that are taking advantage of these trends.

Accounting 101 - The Annual Report

Chapter Goals—

After studying and reviewing this chapter, you will be able to:

- Discuss what an annual report is all about.
- List some of the major sections of an annual report.
- Explain the importance of the auditors' report.

- Locate the section of the annual report where management discusses and analyzes the company's performance.
- Find the business segments from which the company derives its revenues and earnings.

Introduction

Accounting is the language of business and before you begin to use the NAIC Stock Selection Guide (SSG), you need to become acquainted with some of the most frequently used accounting terms. This chapter will examine the content of a company's annual report, which is the primary source of financial information about the corporation. In the next chapter, we will explore the company's balance sheet and income statement. You do not have to become an accountant to invest in stocks, but some knowledge of accounting terminology is very helpful.

The Annual Report: The Primary Source of Company Information

Just like your school, which issues periodic reports on your progress, public companies must send out "report cards" to their shareholders. The annual report is a "report card" summarizing the financial condition of the company and how it is doing.

If you still haven't seen an annual report, ask your librarian to show you one, or call the company. Annual reports can be quite lengthy, almost the size of a small magazine. Some are filled with color pictures and graphics and are very attractive. Public companies are required by law to send out annual reports to their shareholders. The reports provide "bundles" of information about the company, its products or services, its employees, its customers and its future outlook. While all annual reports are not alike, you will find the following major sections in most of them:

- Corporate Profile
- Financial Highlights
- Letter to the Shareholders
- Operational Overview
- Independent Auditors' Report
- Financial Statements
- Notes to Financial Statements
- Management's Discussion and Analysis
- Description of the Company's Business
- Business Segment Information
- Company Directors and Executive Officers
- Five-year Historical Financial Data Summary

Corporate Profile

This section, usually little more than a paragraph, describes the company's business, what it makes or sells. This section may also include information about where the company does business—for example, in the United States, Canada, Europe, etc.

Financial Highlights

One of the more important parts of the annual report is the financial highlights section, which has a brief summary of the "numbers" for the year. Here are many of the numbers that are especially important to shareholders such as profit and loss data. Remember, this is only a summary. More detailed information is contained in the financial statement section.

Letter to the Shareholders

A letter to shareholders (owners of the company) from one of the leaders of the corporation is usually found in the first few pages in the annual report. Sometimes this section is called a "report from management." The person who writes the letter may be the Chief Executive Officer (the CEO), the Chairman of the Board of Directors or the President. Sometimes, one person holds two or more of these titles, for example, President and CEO. The letter to the shareholders gives the corporate leader a chance to communicate with the company owners about the business and its future.

CHAPTER SIXTEEN

Operational Overview

This is also a highlights section. It discusses the company's products or services, as well as significant events or accomplishments during the year. For example, the overview may mention that the company opened 200 new stores or two new manufacturing plants.

Independent Auditors' Report

The auditors are certified public accountants (CPAs) who are responsible for inspecting the company's records ("their books") and offering an "opinion" on how well these records comply with generally accepted accounting rules. The auditors must be "independent," and may not be company employees. If the auditors find the accounting records in order, they issue what is known as a "clean opinion." If they find deviations from acceptable accounting practices, they issue a "qualified opinion." The auditors' "opinion" is critical to shareholders.

Financial Statements

This is the heart of the annual report. As preparation for learning to use the SSG, we shall discuss the two major parts of the financial statement section, (a) the balance sheet and (b) the income statement, in the next chapter.

Notes to Financial Statements

For beginners, this section is difficult to understand. As you become more familiar with accounting terminology, the "notes" will become more relevant.

Management's Discussion & Analysis

This is a detailed section that discusses different segments of the business and how money was made (or lost). It is geared toward money issues.

Description of the Company's Business

This section is a brief description of the nature of the company's business.

Business Segment Information

It is not unusual for a corporation to be engaged in a number of different businesses. This section is important because it lets you know what percentage of the company is dedicated to each business segment. For example, the company may derive 60% of its revenues from Industry A and 40% from Industry B.

Company Directors & Executive Officers

The leaders of the corporation are listed in the annual report. They include (a) the members of the board of directors and (b) the top-level officers. Shareholders elect the board of directors. The directors make broad strategy and policy decisions for the company. But the corporate officers run the business from day to day.

Five-Year Historical Financial Data Summary

This required section summarizes key financial data for the past five years, usually in a table format.

SUMMARY

This chapter has reviewed the major sections of a company's annual report, a basic tool for shareholders. There is a wealth of information in an annual report, and it reveals a great deal about the management of a particular firm. All sections of the annual report are important in evaluating a company's future prospects. In the next chapter, you will learn definitions for key accounting terms that will be useful to you in completing the Stock Selection Guide.

KEY WORDS

ANNUAL REPORT
BUSINESS SEGMENT
   INFORMATION
COMPANY DIRECTORS AND
   EXECUTIVE OFFICERS
CORPORATE PROFILE
DESCRIPTION OF THE
   COMPANY'S BUSINESS
FINANCIAL HIGHLIGHTS
FINANCIAL STATEMENTS
FIVE-YEAR HISTORICAL
   FINANCIAL DATA SUMMARY

INDEPENDENT AUDITORS'
   REPORT
LETTER TO THE
   SHAREHOLDERS
CLEAN OPINION
QUALIFIED OPINION
MANAGEMENT'S DISCUSSION
   AND ANALYSIS
OPERATIONAL OVERVIEW

QUESTIONS & ACTIVITIES

1. Get a copy of an annual report for one of the companies you listed at the end of Chapter 15. Read through the major sections. What does the report tell you about the company's products or services, its business segments, its most recent changes and accomplishments, its financial condition, its future plans, the quality of its management?

   ■

2. Take a ride on the Internet and find a company's Web site. Look at the annual report online. How closely does it conform to the outline presented in this chapter?

   ■

3. What is the meaning of "independent auditors"?

   ■

4. What does the "business segments" section of the annual report tell you and why does this matter to you as an investor?

   ■

5. Why is a company's annual report so important?

CHAPTER SEVENTEEN:

Accounting 101 -
The Income Statement and the Balance Sheet

Chapter Goals–

After studying and reviewing this chapter, you will be able to:

- Distinguish between the time frames of an income statement and a balance sheet.

- Define the term "earnings per share."

- Identify major terms found in the income statement.

- Identify major terms found in the balance sheet.

- Understand the concept of "stockholders' equity."

Introduction

This chapter looks at two major accounting reports: the income statement and the balance sheet. Because accounting gets to be pretty complicated, we are concentrating on the information and terminology that are important to you as a beginning investor. You will also see what these two reports reveal about a company's operations and its financial health.

The Income Statement

The income statement, also called the profit-and-loss statement, represents revenues (sales), expenses and profits (or losses) over a period of time (i.e. one year, one quarter).

The income statement is different from the balance sheet because the income statement shows a "flow" of sales and expenses over time. The balance sheet represents a single point in time. It is a photograph of the company taken on a certain date (i.e. December 31).

Let's look at some of the key items contained in the income statement by referring to the income statement of XYZ Corporation:

XYZ CORPORATION (not real)

December 31, 2002

CONSOLIDATED STATEMENT OF INCOME

(In millions except for per share data)

	2000	2001	2002
Net Sales	$850.5	$947.3	$1075.1
Cost of Goods Sold	620.1	710.3	820.5
Gross Profit	230.4	237.0	254.6
Selling, General, & Administrative Expenses	95.2	89.4	85.7
Operating Income	135.2	147.6	168.9
Other Income (expenses)	3.0	(1.5)	2.6
Income Before Taxes	138.2	146.1	171.5
Income Taxes	55.3	58.4	68.6
Net Income	$82.9	$87.7	$102.9
Earnings Per Share	$1.02	$1.12	$1.31

Net Sales or Revenues

The top line of the income statement is net sales or revenues. It represents total sales during the accounting time period minus products returned and allowances. [Gross sales minus returns and allowances = net sales.] The sales or revenues are from the primary businesses or core operations of the corporation.

Cost of Goods Sold

Cost of goods sold (or cost of sales) refers to the operating expenses directly involved in producing the company's products/services: labor, raw materials and other related expenses.

Gross Profit (or gross profit margin)

This is the company's profit margin after the cost of goods sold is subtracted from company revenues. [Revenues minus CGS = gross profit.]

Selling, General & Administrative Expenses (SG&A)

These are operating expenses not directly associated with making the product. These expenses include sales commissions, legal expenses, accounting expenses, advertising and executive compensation.

Operating Income (profit)

Operating income or profit is what remains from revenues after both CGS and SG&A expenses have been subtracted. Operating income is an important figure for evaluating the success or failure of the company's operations.

The categories which follow are "non-operating" income and expenses.

Other Income

Other income, which is not derived from operations, includes interest and dividends on securities owned by the company, other investment-related activities and gains from selling assets.

Other Expenses

These are non-operating expenses such as interest paid on the company's debts and miscellaneous expenses.

Net Income Before Taxes

Net income before taxes, also called pre-tax income or earnings, is simply net revenues minus all expenses before corporate income taxes.

Net Income

This is the so-called "bottom line." It is net income or net income after taxes.

Earnings per Share (EPS)

This is a very significant figure for investors and one you will use in filling out the Stock Selection Guide (SSG). Earnings per share is the company's net income divided by the number of common stock shares outstanding.

The Balance Sheet

It is called a balance sheet because it balances assets and liabilities (plus shareholder equity).

[Assets = liabilities + shareholders' equity.]

Assets are the properties the company owns and what it has in various accounts. Liabilities are debts (financial claims against the company). Shareholders' equity, the difference between assets and liabilities, consists of capital supplied by stockholders and net profits which were "plowed back" (or retained) in the company for future growth.

Remember that the balance sheet is like a "snapshot" of a company's financial condition. That snapshot will look one way on March 31 and another way on December 31.

This shows you the basic format of a balance sheet. You can evaluate a company's solvency, or ability to pay its debts, by studying the balance sheet.

ZZZ CORPORATION (not real)
December 31, 2002

CONSOLIDATED BALANCE SHEET

(In millions)

ASSETS	2001	2002
Current Assets:		
Cash	$ .8	$ 1.0
Marketable securities	1.0	1.2
Accounts Receivable	83.0	84.0
Inventories	95.6	107.2
Other	1.4	1.6
Total Current Assets	181.8	195.0
Property, plant, and equipment:		
Buildings	300.7	320.1
Machinery & Equipment	550.2	580.1
Less accumulated depreciation	(340.2)	(350.4)
	510.7	549.8
Land	40.0	40.0
Other Assets:	55.2	58.8
Total Assets	$787.7	$843.6
LIABILITIES AND STOCKHOLDERS' EQUITY		
Current Liabilities:		
Accounts payable and accrued expenses	$ 78.0	$ 85.0
Current maturities on long term debt	4.0	4.3
Income taxes payable	8.1	9.5
Total Current Liabilities	90.1	98.8
Long-Term Debt	120.5	125.6
Stockholders' Equity:		
Common stock	81.2	81.8
Retained earnings	495.9	537.4
Total Stockholders' Equity	577.1	619.2
Total Liabilities and Stockholders' Equity	$787.7	$843.6

ASSETS

Current Assets

The term "current assets" refers to assets that could be converted into cash within a year. Current assets are considered very "liquid," meaning they can be liquidated into cash relatively quickly. They are short-term assets, as opposed to longer-term (fixed) assets. In the category of current assets, you will find cash, marketable securities, accounts receivable, inventories and miscellaneous assets. Marketable securities include Treasury bills or notes and other securities with ready markets. Accounts receivable represent dollars owed to the corporation by customers from the sale of goods or services. The term inventory includes raw material inventories (to be used to manufacture goods) and finished product inventories (already manufactured and awaiting sale).

Fixed Assets

Fixed Assets are longer-term assets such as land, buildings and equipment. All of these assets, with the exception of land, are depreciable. Because these assets age, wear out and decline in value, their original cost is "written off" or "depreciated" over a number of years. Remember that fixed assets are recorded on the corporate records at cost and that, after a period of time these figures do not necessarily reflect actual market values.

Other Assets

Other assets may show up on the balance sheet. Prepaid expenses or deferred charges are items the company has paid for in advance, such as a couple months' rent paid ahead of time and prepaid insurance. Some companies list "intangible" assets, assets you can't see or touch, such as patents or copyrights and goodwill. Goodwill is created when one company acquires another company and pays a sum of money over and above the value the company's tangible assets.

Total Assets

[Total assets = current assets + fixed assets + other assets.]

LIABILITIES

Liabilities are amounts of money the corporation owes its creditors.

Current Liabilities

Current liabilities include debts or claims due within one year. The next 12 months' payments on a long-term debt are also included as current liabilities. Current liabilities include accounts payable, notes payable (current portion), accrued expenses, and income taxes payable and other liabilities.

Accounts Payable

Accounts payable are just that, bills the company must pay. These include materials, supplies and services the company has contracted for and usually pays for within 30 days.

Notes Payable

Notes payable refers to the amount due on notes (promissory notes or promises to pay) within the next 12 months.

Accrued Expenses

"Accrued expenses" refers to expenses already incurred, but not yet paid. For example, at the end of an accounting period (i.e. a month) the company may owe money to its employees for days worked, but not yet paid. In other words, the accounting date does not coincide with the end of a pay period. Accrued expenses include wages and salaries, interest on debt and miscellaneous debt.

Income Taxes Payable

Income taxes payable are taxes due on corporate income, but not yet paid.

Long-Term Liabilities

This section of the balance sheet summarizes all long-term liabilities, or debts due after one year. You will see such items as notes payable, bonds (also called debentures) and mortgages.

Total Liabilities

[Current liabilities + long-term liabilities = total liabilities]

Stockholders' (or Shareholders') Equity

The stockholders' equity section represents the amount of money invested by equity owners (both common stock and preferred stockholders) and the amount of net income that was retained in the business. The "retained earnings" are profits "plowed back" into the corporation to invest in future growth. Other terms you will hear used interchangeably with stockholders' equity are "book value" and "net worth."

SUMMARY

A company's income statement and balance sheet measure its financial health. The income statement has key data such as sales (revenues) and earnings (operating, pre-tax and net) for the latest fiscal year. The balance sheet reports the company's assets and liabilities. These accounting reports are tools that help you understand a company's operations and performance. Don't be afraid of the accounting terms. With a little experience, you will feel more comfortable with the language of accounting.

KEY WORDS

NET SALES OR REVENUES	EARNINGS PER SHARE
COST OF GOODS SOLD	CURRENT ASSETS
GROSS PROFIT	FIXED ASSETS
SG&A	OTHER ASSETS
OPERATING PROFIT	TOTAL ASSETS
OTHER INCOME	CURRENT LIABILITIES
OTHER EXPENSES	LONG-TERM LIABILITIES
NET INCOME BEFORE	TOTAL LIABILITIES
TAXES	STOCKHOLDERS' EQUITY
NET INCOME	

QUESTIONS & ACTIVITIES

1. Explain why a balance sheet is a "snapshot or photo" of a company.

   ■

2. What are the key terms found on the income statement?

   ■

3. If a company is said to have a "negative net worth," what are they talking about? What would cause such a situation?

   ■

4. List six major terms found on a balance sheet and explain each.

   ■

5. Using the annual report you obtained from a company of interest to you, list the following:

Total assets	Pre-tax profits
Total liabilities	Net Income
Stockholders' Equity	Earnings per share
Revenues	

Stock Selection Guide Overview

Chapter Goals–

After studying and reviewing this chapter, you will be able to:

- State the two main objectives of the Stock Selection Guide.
- Explain the reasoning behind the SSG.
- Describe the major sections of the SSG.
- Begin to transfer data to the Stock Selection Guide.
- List the pieces of general information requested at the top of SSG, Page 1.
- Explain why the recent quarterly figures are needed.

Introduction

We do not rely simply on outward appearance to judge a person's health. We also want to know what the doctor says based on a whole battery of tests and diagnostic procedures. The Stock Selection Guide (SSG), which you are beginning to use in this chapter, will help you extract hard data on a company and examine it in a systematic way so that you can do your own diagnosis of that company and its prospects for future growth.

What Is The Stock Selection Guide (SSG)?

Background

The Stock Selection Guide was created in the early 1950's, soon after the founding of the NAIC. The chief architect of the SSG was the late George A. Nicholson, Jr. Since that date, the SSG has proved itself a powerful tool for helping investors make better-informed stock investment decisions. The SSG approach is systematic. It walks you through the process of evaluating companies from sales, earnings and profit margin trends to the use of price/earnings ratios. The SSG was not designed for short-term trading action or for highly cyclical stocks. It was designed primarily for growth stocks and long-term investors like you.

Stock Selection Guide ®

NAIC

The most widely used aid to good investment judgment

Company _____ Date _____

Prepared by _____ Data taken from _____

Where traded _____ Major product/service _____

CAPITALIZATION --- Outstanding Amounts		Reference	
Preferred ($M)		% Insiders	% Institution
Common (M Shares)			
Debt ($M)	% to Tot.Cap.	% Potential Dil.	

1 VISUAL ANALYSIS of Sales, Earnings and Price

RECENT QUARTERLY FIGURES

	SALES ($M)	EARNINGS PER SHARE ($)
Latest Quarter		
Year Ago Quarter		
Percentage Change		

(1) Historical Sales Growth _____ %   (3) Historical Earnings Per Share Growth _____ %

(2) Estimated Future Sales Growth _____ %   (4) Estimated Future Earnings Per Share Growth _____ %

Figure 18-01: SSG Page I

Objectives

The SSG has two clear objectives: (1) to help you find companies with a record of consistent growth and (2) to help you determine a reasonable price to pay for the stock of such a company.

The Reasoning Behind the SSG

The NAIC knows that a past record of revenue and earnings growth does not guarantee future growth, but it is a good indicator. If a company's managers have produced consistent growth for five-to-10 years, there is a strong probability that such growth will continue into the future. In forecasting future prices, the SSG relies on past relationships between stock prices and earnings (P/E ratio) and it assumes that similar relationships will continue into the future.

Despite the SSG's usefulness, it should not be considered a "crystal ball." There is no sure thing when you are peering into the future. It is quite possible for two different investors to use the SSG and the same historical data on a company and come to different conclusions about that company and its stock. The stock market has thousands of investors—buyers and sellers—and many different expectations about the future. This is part of what makes the stock market work. Remember, the SSG is an effective tool for sharpening the stock selection process, but you must learn its strengths and limitations. And you must add your own judgment.

Additional information on the SSG may be found in NAIC's *Stock Selection Handbook,* by Bonnie Biafore.

How Is the SSG Organized?

The Stock Selection Guide and Report is comprised of four pages to be filled in by the investor. Page 1 has three areas: general information on the company (at top of the page), recent quarterly sales and earning figures and Section 1, "Visual Analysis," a graph for charting sales, earnings and price.

Page 2 has: Section 2, "Evaluating Management," trends in two key financial ratios; Section 3, "Price-Earnings History," to help you calculate the price to earnings ratio; Section 4, "Evaluating Risk and Reward," critical to determining whether you should buy a particular stock; and Section 5, "Five-Year Potential," for estimating the potential five-year return.

Pages three and four of the SSG contain eight questions which you answer to help you determine whether a stock is an appropriate purchase based on your goals.

When you are transferring data to the SSG, you should rely on only one investment information source and should not mix sources such as Value Line and Standard & Poor's. There are small differences in how they calculate certain figures. For illustration purposes, we shall use information on a "real live company," Johnson & Johnson, the world's largest and most comprehensive health care company. This SSG example is for educational purposes only, and should not be considered an investment recommendation.

Let's begin with Page 1 of the SSG, shown on page 113.

General Information (Top Right, SSG Page 1)

The block at the top of the page is for general information about the company you are evaluating. It is basic descriptive information for reference purposes:

- Company Name
- Date
- Prepared by
- Data taken from
- Where traded
- Major product/service
- Capitalization
- % ownership by company insiders and institutions

An example of the general information for Johnson & Johnson is shown on the next page. The date is the date of your study. It is important for future reference to have the date in case you want to compare this study with a new study of the same stock at a later time. The "prepared by" space is for the name or initials of the person preparing the SSG.

Note the source ("data taken from") of your data. This may be a corporate annual report, Value Line or Standard & Poor's. It could be a source downloaded from an online computer service (such as NAIC's Online Premium Service). For consistency purposes, your data should come from one source only, not a combination of sources.

"Where traded" means the stock market where the company's stock trades (NYSE, NASDAQ, AMEX). Your information source will tell you this and it will also tell you the major products or services produced by the company. JNJ is the abbreviation or ticker symbol for Johnson & Johnson on the NYSE.

The term capitalization means how the corporation is financed, through common stock, preferred stock, long-term debt or a combination. There are spaces for both common stock and preferred stock (if any). In Value Line, this information is found in the block entitled "Capital Structure." "Debt" can mean either total debt or long-term debt. Value Line reports total debt amounts, including long-term debt.

Company debt is a factor you should not overlook. It adds risk to a company's earnings performance because the interest payments on that debt must be paid whether a company has a good year or not. More meaningful than the amount of debt in dollars, is the debt percentage, the ratio of debt to total capitalization, which you can find in Value Line. At JNJ, the 9/30/02 long-term debt as a percentage of total capitalization was 9%.

As a general rule for manufacturing firms, the debt level should not be more than 33% (1/3) of total capitalization. To determine if a larger debt is acceptable, you should check the historical debt of that company and compare it with the debt of other companies in the same industry.

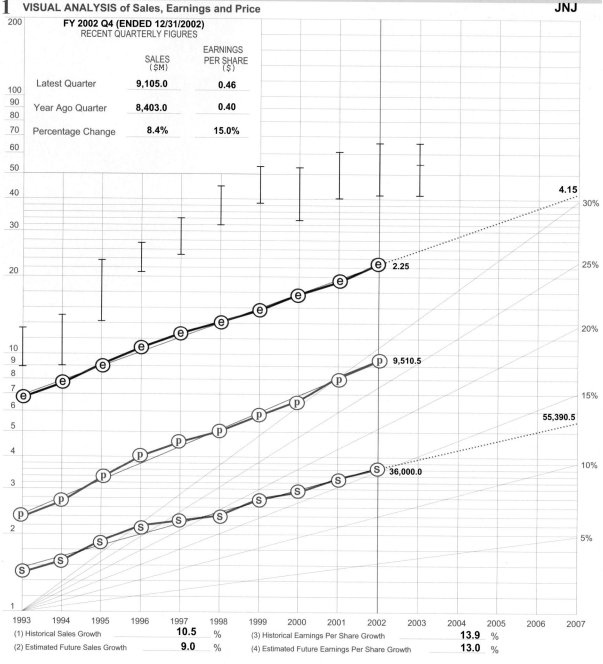

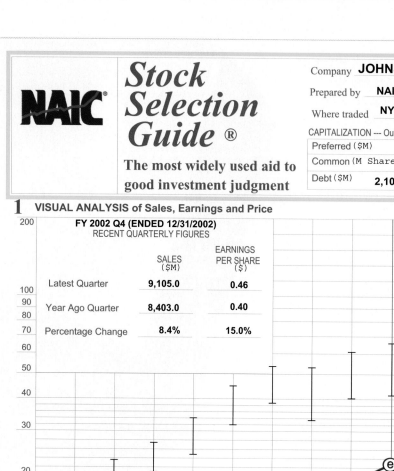

NAIC®

Stock Selection Guide ®

The most widely used aid to good investment judgment

Company	**JOHNSON & JOHNSON**		Date **01/17/03**
Prepared by	**NAIC**	Data taken from	**Value Line**
Where traded	**NYSE**	Major product/service	**Pharmaceuticals**

CAPITALIZATION --- Outstanding Amounts		Reference **pg. 213**	
Preferred ($M)	**0.0**	% Insiders	% Institution
Common (M Shares)	**2,970.6**	**0.2**	**61.9**
Debt ($M) **2,102.0**	% to Tot.Cap. **9.0**	% Potential Dil.	**None**

1 VISUAL ANALYSIS of Sales, Earnings and Price
JNJ

FY 2002 Q4 (ENDED 12/31/2002)
RECENT QUARTERLY FIGURES

	SALES ($M)	EARNINGS PER SHARE ($)
Latest Quarter	9,105.0	0.46
Year Ago Quarter	8,403.0	0.40
Percentage Change	8.4%	15.0%

4.15

2.25

9,510.5

55,390.5

36,000.0

1993 1994 1995 1996 1997 1998 1999 2000 2001 2002 2003 2004 2005 2006 2007

(1) Historical Sales Growth **10.5** % (3) Historical Earnings Per Share Growth **13.9** %
(2) Estimated Future Sales Growth **9.0** % (4) Estimated Future Earnings Per Share Growth **13.0** %

Figure 18-02: JNJ SSG Page I - General Information

The box entitled "% Insiders" refers to the percentage of common stock owned by officers and directors of the company. This figure is found in Value Line in the text of the paragraph entitled "Business." It is a good sign when insiders own shares because they are risking some of their own money on the future of the company.

The amount of stock held by institutional investors (mutual funds, banks, pension funds, etc.) is found in Value Line under "Institutional Decisions" (near the upper left corner). For JNJ, we can see that, as of 2Q (2nd quarter) 2002, institutions held 1.837 billion of the 2.970 billion shares outstanding (or 61.9%).

Another box in this section is called "Potential Dilution." The term "Dilution" means reducing the value of the shares held by existing shareholders by issuing additional shares at less than the current market price. In other words, net earnings are divided by more shares outstanding. Dilution is a negative for existing shareholders. Since 1997, diluted earnings per share are clearly reported to investors (as shown in the Value Line footnote). New investors should concentrate on the diluted EPS data for their SSG analysis. Thus, in general, the "Potential Dilution" box can be left blank.

Recent Quarterly Results (Middle Left, Page 1, SSG)

Another area on Page 1 of the SSG is a box entitled "recent quarterly figures." This section is used to record the latest quarterly revenues and earnings per share figures, compared to the same quarter one year ago. In addition, the percentage of change is calculated.

Under section heading, it is a good idea to record the date of the most recent quarterly data (i.e. December, 2002). Value Line provides this data. If you were studying a stock in mid-January 2003, you may not have the data for the 4th quarter of 2002. Thus, in this section of the SSG, you can use the estimated Value Line numbers for the 4Q 2002 revenues and EPS and calculate the percentage change from 4Q 2002. Why is this important? It gives you the latest performance data and keeps you up-to-date on the company's current environment. It also alerts you to a possible change in direction. You calculate change percentages in the following way:

most recent quarter data minus year ago quarter data / year ago quarter data	X 100 = % change

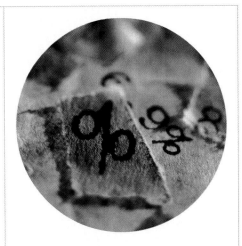

"Wall Street" (i.e. the institutional investor) is obsessed with quarterly data and buys and sells based on quarterly expectations. This stimulates short-term fluctuations in the stock prices and creates buying opportunities. Quarterly financial information is available when the company releases this information and it can be found in the financial press (*The Wall Street Journal,* etc.) and on various sites on the Internet. Some companies will even send this information to your e-mail address, if you request it.

You can see an example of the SSG "Recent Quarterly Figures" for JNJ on Page 118.

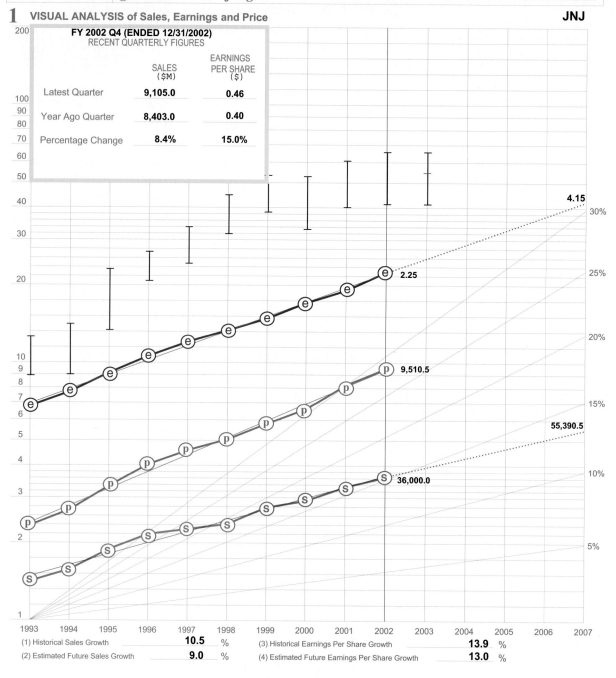

Figure 18-03: JNJ SSG Page I - Quarterly Results

SUMMARY

First-time investors are often confused about the factors needed to select appropriately priced common stocks for their portfolio. The Stock Selection Guide offers a systematic approach to finding and selecting good growth companies at reasonable prices. This chapter explains some of the general information on Page 1 of the SSG.

KEY WORDS

FIVE-YEAR POTENTIAL SECTION
DEBT AS PERCENT TO TOTAL CAPITALIZATION
EVALUATING MANAGEMENT SECTION
EVALUATING RISK AND REWARD SECTION
GENERAL INFORMATION SECTION
LONG-TERM DEBT
NAIC'S *STOCK SELECTION HANDBOOK*
PRICE-EARNINGS HISTORY
RECENT QUARTERLY FIGURES SECTION
SHARES OUTSTANDING
STOCK SELECTION GUIDE (SSG)
TOTAL DEBT
VISUAL ANALYSIS SECTION

QUESTIONS & ACTIVITIES

1. List the five major sections of the SSG.

   ■

2. On the blank SSG provided in this chapter, fill in the top right corner with the necessary information for a company of your choice.

   ■

3. Fill in the "Recent Quarterly Results" box for the same company as in question #1.

   ■

4. It is permissible to mix data from different investment sources (i.e. Value Line and S&P) when completing the SSG. (True or False)

   ■

5. The SSG was designed primarily for investing long term in growth-oriented stocks. (True or False)

   ■

6. The SSG will aid an investor who is trying to determine short-term trading ranges of a stock. (True or False)

   ■

7. What is the major reason for completing the SSG?

   ■

8. The SSG is more fully explained in the NAIC's *Stock Selection Handbook* (True or False)

CHAPTER NINETEEN:

Plotting the Data

Chapter Goals–

After studying and reviewing this chapter, you will be able to:

- Explain the basic concept of a semi-logarithmic (semi-log) graph.

- Discuss why you plot sales, earnings and price information data on the SSG graph.

- Plot 10 years of a company's sales, earnings per share (EPS) and prices on the SSG graph.

- List some explanations of sales and EPS trends.

- Visualize the "big picture" (graph) of a company's performance.

Introduction

This chapter will familiarize you with the SSG graph, teaching you why it is important, what the numbers mean and how to plot data on it. The primary objective of the graph is to estimate historical and future growth rates for revenues and earnings per share (EPS). Growth rates are the primary drivers behind common stock prices. You will quickly see that this complicated looking graph is easy to use and it will become one of your primary investment tools.

The SSG Graph– Visual Analysis of Sales, Earnings & Prices

You are probably scratching your head right now and saying, "What in the world is this crazy graph with all the lines?" You will use the graph to plot a company's sales (revenues), earnings per share and common stock prices for the past 10 years (if they are available for that length of time).

The Stock Selection Guide is on semi-logarithmic graph paper (also called semi-log paper or a ratio chart). The beauty of semi-log paper is the fact that it allows you to record dollar amounts, but to plot and study them as percentages of change over a period of time. This means you can compare the rate of change of companies even if they are different sizes.

You will plot three key kinds of corporate data:

1. Total sales (revenues).
2. Earnings per share.
3. High and low annual common stock prices for the past 10 years (if available).

Once plotted, these data are used to estimate the historical growth rates of the revenues and earnings per share. The historical growth rates, along with the recent quarterly growth rates, will help you project future growth rates for the next five years.

Note: When you manually prepare a SSG, you use the three key corporate data above. In our JNJ illustration you will see a 4th trend line, pre-tax profits, which are normally included automatically when you use SSG software, like Investor's Toolkit.

How to Read the Graph

On the graph, the vertical lines represent years. The horizontal lines represent dollar amounts. The shrinking spaces between numbers in the left margin reflect the fact that, as the numbers increase, it takes a greater numerical change to produce the same percentage of change. [Example: If you start with a dollar, it only takes a dollar to double your money. But if you start with 10 dollars, you will need 10 dollars to produce the same percentage of gain!] The number of horizontal lines varies with the type of NAIC tool you are using. The manual NAIC SSG form contains more horizontal lines than do the SSG software products (i.e. *NAIC Classic* and *Toolkit*). While the number of lines may differ, the measurements and concepts remain the same in both the manual version and the software versions.

Vertical lines:

- Represent years.
- The first 10 years show historical data (the **bold** vertical line and the 9 lines to the left of it).
- Last five years (to the right of the **bold** vertical line) project future growth.

Horizontal lines:

- Represent numerical figures.
- Run in two and a fraction cycles: from 1-10, from 10-100 and from 100-200.
- Have 5 lines between 1-4, 10-40 and 100-200, so that the value of each line is two.
- Have no lines between 4-10 and 40-100, so that you pick the appropriate placement for your data point (a .45 or 4.5 could be placed between the 4 and 5 lines or the 40 and 50 lines)
- Carry the same value across the page.

Why Do You Chart Data on the SSG Graph?

The sales and earnings are plotted in order to find the average rate (percentage) of growth over the past 10 years. This will help you make a reasonable growth projection for the next five years. Revenue and earnings have a significant influence on common stock prices. So, you will carry the projected earnings figures over to Page 2 of the SSG, and you will use them to help you forecast the high price of the company's stock in the next five years. Growth is the principal determinant of stock price increases. Where consistent growth is present, a consistent increase in price is almost certain to follow.

Also plotted on the graph are the high and low prices of the company's common stock for each entered year so you can see how well the company's stock has done in the past 10 years. If it has done well, it will probably continue to do so in the next five years.

You chart the past because you want to evaluate the possible future growth of the company. You are not buying the past. You are buying the future. It just so happens that looking back is often one of the best ways of looking ahead. Of course, there are other factors to weigh, too–the future of the industry the company is in, the competition in that industry and the condition of the economy as a whole. Studying the past is only one way of sizing up the future. At one time, buggy whips and iceboxes were great industries and they probably had excellent track records, but something came along and changed everything.

When the SSG graph is filled in, you will have a picture of a company's sales, pre-tax profits, earnings per share (EPS) and stock price trends—and a good overview of management's accomplishments. If you have less than 10 years to work with, you should give more attention to the present state of the business cycle, and be more conservative. At least a five-year history is needed to produce a true evaluation on the SSG and a representative picture of management's accomplishments.

How to Plot the Data

Number the Years at the Bottom of the Page

Sometimes corporations base their financial data on a fiscal year that often does not correspond to a calendar year. The fiscal year may run, for example, from July 1 to June 30. When deciding which years to use on the graph, note when the fiscal year ends. You can find this in Value Line. This will help you determine the most recent year (bold vertical line) to plot on your graph.

If the company has already issued three quarterly reports in the current year, add the estimated fourth quarter (Value Line) to complete the year. This is what we did in the Johnson & Johnson SSG example. Recent information is important. If only one quarterly report is out for the current year, use the last fully reported year. It may also be best to use the last given year if two quarterly reports are out, but note if increases are expected in the next two quarters. Do not hesitate to use estimates, but remember that estimates are guesses and may not work out. We used estimated fourth quarter data from VL for JNJ.

Plotting Historical Sales

Now let's use the left scale of the graph and the horizontal lines. Johnson & Johnson's sales (revenues) for 2002 were estimated at $36,000 million ($36.0 billion). Sales are usually represented in millions of dollars, but you may move the decimal as many places as you need to arrive at workable numbers. We plotted $36,000 million in the 1-10 cycle just above 3.6. The graph of revenue changes over a 10-year period and the projection of revenues into the future will look the same in either cycle.

Here are some simple guidelines for plotting sales:

- Scan to see where the sales numbers will fit in the cycles.

- Use pencil (guess why?). Experts sometimes erase, too.

- Distinguish sales from earnings by using a different color or some other identifying mark for each.

- When possible, plot sales and earnings in a different cycle. If you avoid merging lines, the graph will be easier to read.

- Plot prices close to and above earnings per share data.

Historical sales (revenues) for Johnson & Johnson are plotted on the Stock Selection Guide on page 124. The data are derived from Value Line.

Some Reasons for Sales Trend Changes Might Be:

- New or improved products or services.

- A record of introducing successful products or services.

- An upturn from a recession.

- Purchase of another company. If so, check to see whether the company has made any successful purchases in the past. That success indicates that this purchase will probably succeed, too.

- A stagnating market for products or services, with little possibility of future expansion, causing sales to level off.

- An expanding market for products or services, causing sales to rise.

- A market that has expanded geographically.

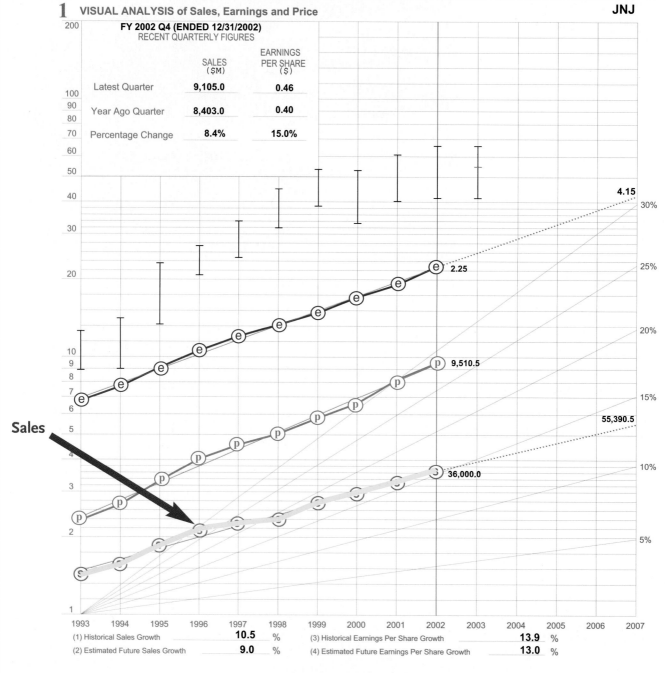

Figure 19-01: Sales History

Plotting Historical Earnings per Share

Earnings per share are given in dollars and cents. In 2002, the diluted earnings per share for JNJ were estimated at $2.25. You could plot this number a quarter of the way between 20 and 30, and then work with earnings less than a dollar per share in the seven to nine cycle range. The 2001 earnings per share, $1.91, for example, should be located between the implied 18 line and the 20 line.

- Scan to see where the earnings numbers will fit in the cycles.

- Be sure to use earnings figures for the same years used for sales.

- If you are graphing a fast growing-company, the sales and earnings will have to start in the lower cycle in order to fit on the graph.

Ideally, you want to see past earnings per share growth closely parallel to sales growth. Because earnings come from sales, the two lines should move up and down together. When they do not, you should try to figure out why.

Some reasons earnings might be growing more slowly than sales are:

1. Declining profit margins.

2. Increasing number of shares of stock outstanding, dividing earnings among more shares.

3. Declining unit sales from increasing competition

Some reasons earnings might be growing faster than sales are:

1. Increasing profit margins because management is reducing expenses.

2. Decrease in number of shares of stock outstanding, so that earnings are divided among fewer shares (i.e., company stock repurchase plan).

3. Reductions in the size of the workforce, fewer workers to pay.

Earnings per share for Johnson & Johnson are plotted on the SSG on page 126. The figures are derived from Value Line.

Plotting Historical Price Bars

Find common stock prices for the same years as you used for sales and earnings. If price span allows, plot the high-low price bars in the same cycle above the earnings data. This will paint a clearer picture of how the earnings affect the stock prices.

- Note the low price for each year.

- Represent this low price on the graph with a short mark.

- Note the high price for each year.

- Represent this high price on the graph with a short mark.

- Connect these two marks to form the price bars.

Price bars show how much movement (volatility) there is in the price each year. This could be an indicator of risk in future years.

Price bars for Johnson & Johnson are plotted on the SSG on Page 127. The figures are derived from Value Line.

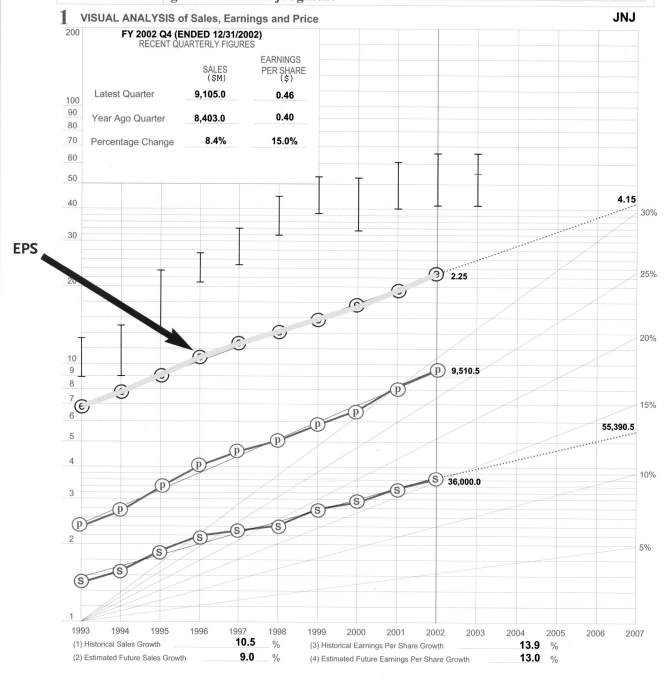

Stock Selection Guide ®

The most widely used aid to good investment judgment

Company **JOHNSON & JOHNSON**   Date **01/17/03**

Prepared by **NAIC**   Data taken from **Value Line**

Where traded **NYSE**   Major product/service **Pharmaceuticals**

CAPITALIZATION --- Outstanding Amounts   Reference **pg. 213**

		% Insiders	% Institution
Preferred ($M)	**0.0**		
Common (M Shares)	**2,970.6**	**0.2**	**61.9**
Debt ($M) **2,102.0**	% to Tot.Cap. **9.0**	% Potential Dil.	**None**

1 VISUAL ANALYSIS of Sales, Earnings and Price   **JNJ**

FY 2002 Q4 (ENDED 12/31/2002)
RECENT QUARTERLY FIGURES

	SALES ($M)	EARNINGS PER SHARE ($)
Latest Quarter	**9,105.0**	**0.46**
Year Ago Quarter	**8,403.0**	**0.40**
Percentage Change	**8.4%**	**15.0%**

EPS

4.15

2.25

9,510.5

55,390.5

36,000.0

1993 1994 1995 1996 1997 1998 1999 2000 2001 2002 2003 2004 2005 2006 2007			
(1) Historical Sales Growth	**10.5** %	(3) Historical Earnings Per Share Growth	**13.9** %
(2) Estimated Future Sales Growth	**9.0** %	(4) Estimated Future Earnings Per Share Growth	**13.0** %

Figure 19-02: Earnings Per Share History

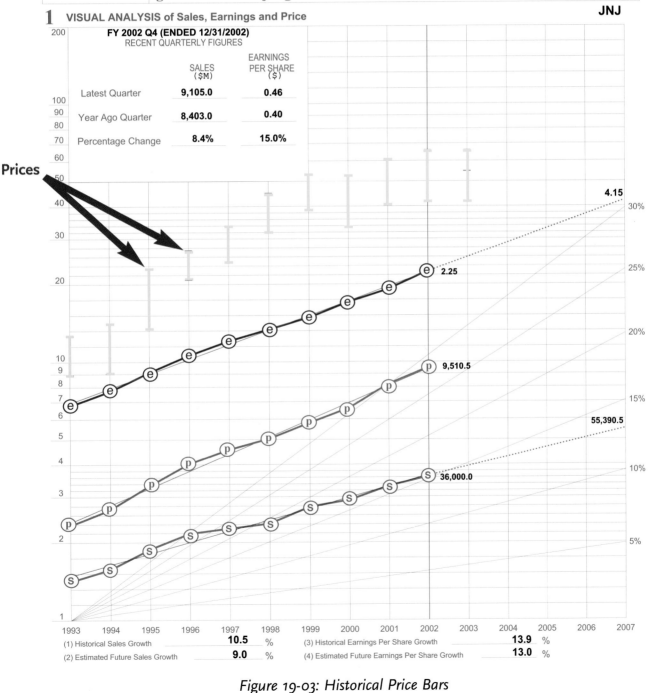

Stock Selection Guide ®

The most widely used aid to good investment judgment

Company	JOHNSON & JOHNSON		Date	01/17/03
Prepared by	NAIC		Data taken from	Value Line
Where traded	NYSE		Major product/service	Pharmaceuticals

CAPITALIZATION --- Outstanding Amounts		Reference	pg. 213	
Preferred ($M)	0.0	% Insiders	% Institution	
Common (M Shares)	2,970.6	0.2	61.9	
Debt ($M)	2,102.0	% to Tot.Cap. 9.0	% Potential Dil.	None

JNJ

1 VISUAL ANALYSIS of Sales, Earnings and Price

FY 2002 Q4 (ENDED 12/31/2002)
RECENT QUARTERLY FIGURES

	SALES ($M)	EARNINGS PER SHARE ($)
Latest Quarter	9,105.0	0.46
Year Ago Quarter	8,403.0	0.40
Percentage Change	8.4%	15.0%

Prices

4.15

2.25

9,510.5

55,390.5

36,000.0

1993 1994 1995 1996 1997 1998 1999 2000 2001 2002 2003 2004 2005 2006 2007

(1) Historical Sales Growth	10.5 %	(3) Historical Earnings Per Share Growth	13.9 %
(2) Estimated Future Sales Growth	9.0 %	(4) Estimated Future Earnings Per Share Growth	13.0 %

Figure 19-03: Historical Price Bars

127

SUMMARY

You are plotting the sales, EPS and price data on the graph to observe trends and measure growth rates. If you use NAIC SSG software, these trend lines are automatically inputted, along with the pre-tax profit trend line. In the next chapter you will learn how to draw trend lines and estimate growth rates.

KEY WORDS

CALENDAR YEAR
FISCAL YEAR
PLOT
PRICE BARS
VOLATILITY
SEMI-LOGARITHMIC
EARNINGS PER SHARE
SALES
COMMON STOCK PRICES

PROJECTS

1. Explain why the graph is on semi-log paper.

   ■

2. How many years of a company's history must you have to produce a meaningful evaluation on the SSG?

   ■

3. Give some reasons why a company's sales may have increased in the past. Can you think of reasons other than the ones listed?

   ■

4. Give some reasons why earnings might grow more slowly than sales. Can you think of reasons not in the list?

   ■

5. Why are you looking at the past when you are really buying the future?

   ■

6. Choose a company that you want to study and plot sales, earnings and price bar data on the SSG graph.

Trend Lines & Growth Rates

Chapter Goals–

After studying and reviewing this chapter, you will be able to:

- Explain the importance of historical trends lines on the SSG graph.

- Discuss the significance of "outliers."

- List the four methods used to draw trend lines.

- Differentiate between the four trend line methods.

- Draw trend lines (for a stock of your choice) and estimate the historical growth rates.

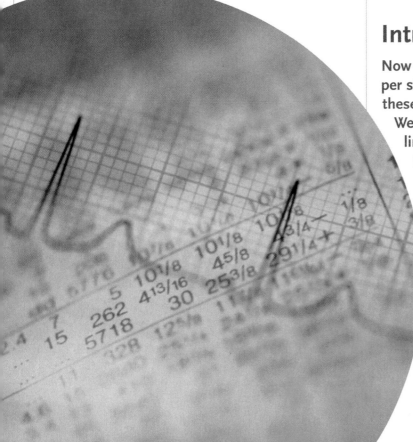

Introduction

Now that we have plotted historical sales, earnings per share and stock prices, our next step is to use these data to estimate historical growth rates. We'll look at four methods of drawing trend lines and estimating historical growth rates. Remember, our objective here is to determine the company's past performance in terms of revenues and EPS, and then use our judgment to estimate a future growth rate. Once again, we'll be working on the SSG graph.

How to Estimate Historical Growth Rates

You may have noticed that this section of the SSG is called "Visual Analysis of Sales, Earnings and Price." With the data plotted on the semi-log chart (graph), we want to "view" the trends of these three variables.

This visual analysis is a crucial step in the SSG approach to stock selection, but the methods used for estimating historical growth rates are reasonably easy to master. Our main objective is to identify consistent trends in a company's sales, EPS and stock price. After identifying and drawing the trend lines, we want to "quantify" them in terms of a growth rate.

Ideally, you want to have a company's 10-year performance history to plot on the graph. Because some companies are relatively new, you may have to work with a shorter history. You should not use a company with less than five years of financial data.

Before you go to the next step, look at the "data points" on the graph to see whether there are any years where the data points seem to be out of line (an "outlier"). An outlier looks abnormal in relationship to the rest of the data. It may be a year where EPS was up or down significantly, probably due to an unusual (non-recurring) event. Although there are no "outliers" in the examples in this chapter, you should watch for them in order to evaluate them.

You should also do some research to see if you can find the reason for the year's abnormal data. Was there a strike by a labor union? A gain resulting from the sale of a subsidiary? And you certainly want to know whether there were any significant changes in the company's operations at the time in question.

With the data plotted on the graph, we shall try to identify trends by drawing trend lines which best represent all the data points for each variable (sales, EPS). We use a ruler to draw a trend line that represents an average of the data points. There are four different methods for drawing the trend line. You should know when to use each method, but typically, you will select only one. Your historical trend line is drawn from the vertical line on the far left (10-year-old data) to the bold line (current year). Let's look at the four basic methods of drawing trend lines on Page 131.

The Inspection or Best Judgment Method

This is the most commonly used method. You simply look at the historical data for one variable and (excluding outliers) draw a line that best represents the overall trend. In other words, you are "eyeballing" the data and using your best judgment to draw a representative trend line.

The Peak Period Method

This method should be used only when deep peaks and valleys have appeared on the graph. You have what is known as a cyclical pattern and the company you are evaluating is a cyclical company. Place your ruler at the most recent peak (most current years) and drop down to the next peak (earlier years). Draw a line that connects these points.

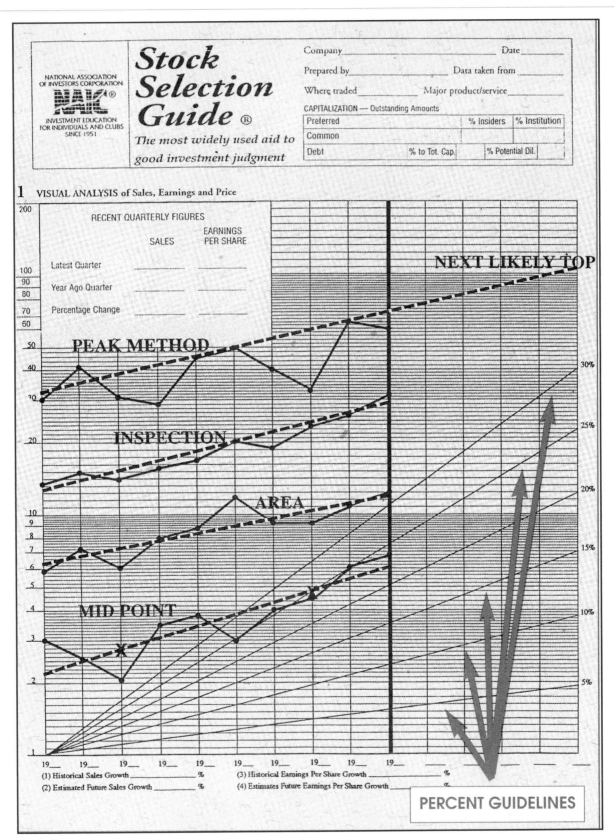

Figure 20-01: Drawing Trend Lines

The Mid Point Method

This method uses mathematical averages and is fairly easy to calculate:

1. Calculate the average of the most recent five data points for sales and EPS, respectively.

2. Plot that number on the graph at the middle of the most recent five-year period.

3. Calculate the average for the previous five years.

4. Plot that number at the middle year of that five-year period.

5. Draw a line through those two points going from the left margin to the current year (bold line).

6. If you are working with fewer than 10 years, find the averages for the first half of those years and the last half and use those two averages to draw the trend line.

The Area Method

The objective of this method is to draw a trend line through the middle of the data points and divide the area they cover in half. The area enclosed by data points above the line is roughly equal to the area enclosed by data points below the line.

Choosing a Method

You will use one of these four methods to represent the growth rate of the data you have plotted. After a little experience, you will quickly recognize which method to use. Remember, the purpose of the trend line is to show the average growth rate of the data points you have plotted. If the points follow a consistent upward pattern, you will have more confidence in your trend line. But if the data points are scattered "all over the board," your trend line will be more difficult to draw and you will not have as much confidence in it.

Remember, the trend line represents an average and the slope of the line depicts an estimated historical growth rate. A line that is steeper than another line reflects faster growth.

The Next Step

After drawing the trend line, you can now read the historical growth rate by comparing the trend line you have drawn with the graph's pre-drawn percentage growth lines (percent guidelines, marked 5%, 10%, 15%, 20%, 25% and 30%). Here's what you do:

1. With a ruler, measure the distance between the point where your trend line crosses the left margin line and the bottom of the graph. Note that measurement.

2. Go to the point where your trend line intersects the bold line (the current year).

3. Measure down from that point the same distance measured in step 1.

4. Mark that point on the graph.

5. Estimate where this point is located between the guidelines (for example, halfway between 15% and 20% = 17.5% annual growth).

6. This is the average annual historical growth rate.

You do this exercise for both revenues and EPS and record the numbers on lines (1) and (3) at the bottom of Page 1 of the SSG. Before we can complete Page 1 of the SSG with our projection lines for revenues and EPS, we need to complete Section 2, Evaluating Management (next chapter).

An example of estimating historical growth rates for Johnson & Johnson is found on Pages 134 and 135.

TREND LINES

- Refer to historical data
- Measure rate of growth
- Must be drawn from left hand margin to 10 year line
- Indicate direction of a trend
- Does not have to be drawn through the last point plotted

1 TREND LINES

To determine past growth rate, measure from where the trend line crosses the left margin down to the bottom line of the graph. Measure the same distance down from where the line crosses the 10 year line. Read the growth rate. This shows 23%. Do **not** use for the projection.

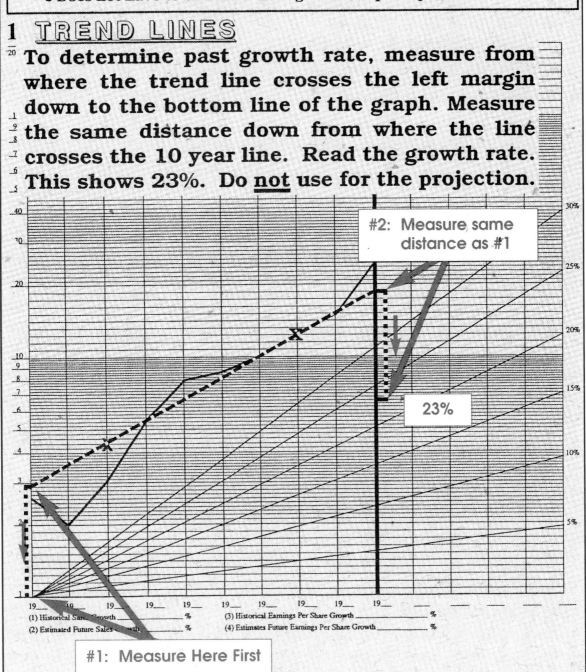

#2: Measure same distance as #1

23%

#1: Measure Here First

(1) Historical Sales Growth _____ %
(2) Estimated Future Sales Growth _____ %
(3) Historical Earnings Per Share Growth _____ %
(4) Estimates Future Earnings Per Share Growth _____ %

Figure 20-02: Measuring for Historical Growth Rates

133

Stock Selection Guide ®

The most widely used aid to good investment judgment

Company	**JOHNSON & JOHNSON**		Date **01/17/03**	
Prepared by	**NAIC**		Data taken from	**Value Line**
Where traded	**NYSE**		Major product/service	**Pharmaceuticals**

CAPITALIZATION --- Outstanding Amounts		Reference **pg. 213**	
Preferred ($M)	**0.0**	% Insiders	% Institution
Common (M Shares)	**2,970.6**	**0.2**	**61.9**
Debt ($M) **2,102.0**	% to Tot.Cap. **9.0**	% Potential Dil.	**None**

1 VISUAL ANALYSIS of Sales, Earnings and Price   **JNJ**

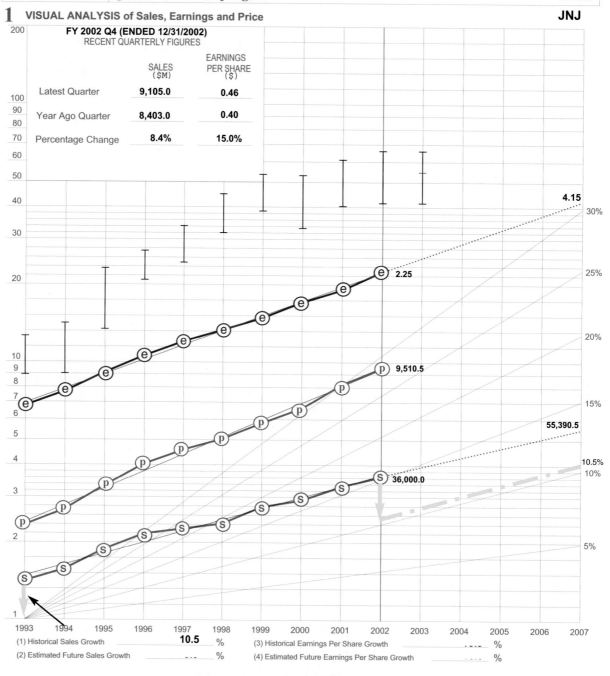

FY 2002 Q4 (ENDED 12/31/2002)
RECENT QUARTERLY FIGURES

	SALES ($M)	EARNINGS PER SHARE ($)
Latest Quarter	9,105.0	0.46
Year Ago Quarter	8,403.0	0.40
Percentage Change	8.4%	15.0%

(1) Historical Sales Growth _____ **10.5** %
(2) Estimated Future Sales Growth _____ %
(3) Historical Earnings Per Share Growth _____ %
(4) Estimated Future Earnings Per Share Growth _____ %

Figure 20-03: Historical Sales Growth Rate

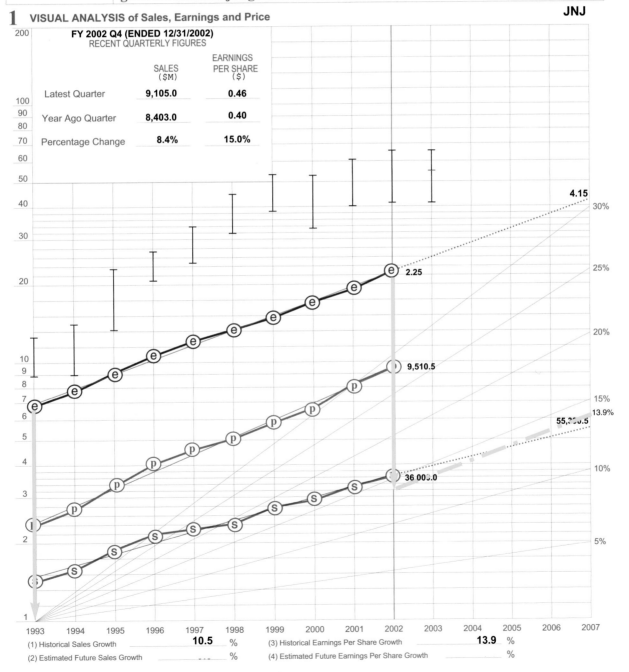

Figure 20-04: Historical Earnings Per Share Growth Rate

SUMMARY

With the data plotted, your mission is to estimate the historical growth rates of revenues and EPS by drawing trend lines. The trend line indicates an average growth rate. You learned four methods for drawing trend lines on the SSG graph. With two simple measurements, you can use the pre-drawn percentage lines to determine annual growth rates. Remember, you should not just take the historical trend line and project it into the future. Your judgment is needed. Chapter 22 will show you how the projection lines are determined.

KEY WORDS

INSPECTION OR BEST JUDGMENT METHOD
CYCLICAL
PEAK PERIOD METHOD
MID POINT METHOD
AREA METHOD
PRE-DRAWN PERCENTAGE GROWTH LINES (GUIDELINES)
OUTLIERS

PROJECTS

1. Explain why you draw trend lines on the SSG graph.

   ■

2. Explain each of the four methods for drawing trend lines.

   ■

3. Take the company you have been studying from prior chapters and draw the most appropriate trend lines for sales and EPS. Calculate their historical growth rates.

   ■

4. The historical trend lines should be used as the future projection lines. (True or False)

   ■

5. Abnormal data, or "outliers," should be taken out of the trend line calculation. (True or False)

Evaluating Management

Chapter Goals–

After studying and reviewing this chapter, you will be able to:

- Compute pre-tax profits on sales from Value Line data.

- Determine if the pre-tax profit on sales is growing.

- Determine if management is controlling costs.

- Analyze the percent earned on equity for a company.

- Explain why pre-tax profit margins and percent earned on equity are important factors to consider.

Introduction

Section 2 of the SSG is a tool to help you evaluate a company's management by examining two key ratios: (1) the ratio of pre-tax profit to sales (revenue) and (2) the ratio of net earnings to equity. A good profit margin and a good return on the equity capital invested in the company are both signs that the company is well managed.

Section 2

The first thing to do in this section is to fill in the years you are examining. Use the same years as you used on the graph (SSG Section 1).

Section 2A: Ratio of Pre-Tax Profit to Sales

This ratio of pre-tax profit to sales is an indicator of how well management is controlling costs and revenues and producing stable or increasing pre-tax profit margins. To compute this ratio, divide the company's pre-tax profit by that year's sales figure. And to express that ratio as a percentage, multiply by 100.

In Section 2A, you fill in these percentages for each of the years you are studying. Where do you get the information to calculate these percentages? From investment data service companies like Value Line and Standard & Poor's, or from the company's annual report.

As we are specifically using the Value Line report for our data, we'll look at it.

Value Line does not report pre-tax profits, but it does give you net profit (after taxes) and the tax rate and you can use that information to figure out profit before taxes. The formula to compute pre-tax profit is:

$$\frac{Net\ Profit}{(1-Tax\ Rate)} = Pre\text{-}Tax\ Profit$$

The reason for focusing on pre-tax profit rather than after-tax profit is the fact that management exercises more control over pre-tax profit. After all, the government sets corporate tax rates and plays an important role in determining net (after tax) profit.

Here are step-by-step calculations for deriving the 2001 pre-tax profit for Johnson & Johnson from the net profit figure provided by Value Line.

2001

$$\frac{\$5{,}885\ million\ (net\ profit)}{1-.282\ (tax\ rate\ as\ a\ decimal)\ or\ .718} = \$8{,}196.4\ million\ (pre\text{-}tax\ profit)$$

And these are the calculations to determine the percent of pre-tax profit on sales.

$$\frac{\$8{,}196.4\ million\ (pre\text{-}tax\ profit)}{\$33{,}004\ million\ (sales)} = .248\ or\ 24.8\%\ (percent\ of\ profit\ on\ sales)$$

Profit Margin Trend

After you have completed these calculations, you will want to examine the profit margin trend, especially for the last five years. Average your percentage figures for the past five years and place that number in the "Last Five-Year Average" box. Then, observe whether last year's profit margin figure is higher or lower than the five-year average. A higher number indicates that the company is continuing to grow and this is shown by a check or an arrow in the "Up" box.

A 10-year example of percent of pre-tax profits on sales calculated for Johnson & Johnson is found on Page 140.

Section 2B: Percent Earned on Equity

The percent earned on equity is an indicator of management's ability to earn an appropriate return on the capital supplied by common stockholders (through their stock purchases and through net profits plowed back into the company).

Just to refresh your memory, the term "equity" is an accounting term used to mean stockholders' equity. It is found by subtracting total liabilities from total assets. Stockholders' equity is also called "book value" or "net worth."

The numbers in 2B are calculated by dividing EPS by book value per share. If you use Standard & Poor's or Value Line, this calculation has already been done for you. S&P shows it as "% Ret. on Equity," and Value Line as "Return on Shr. (Shareholders') Equity." The calculation of the percent earned on equity may vary slightly among investment reporting services (S&P, Value Line and the company itself). Again, when completing a SSG, you should take all of your data from the same source to make sure they are consistent. Do not mix and match data from different sources.

Fill in the percentage earned on equity for each year in the appropriate box. As in 2A, take an average of the last five years. Compare last year's figure to that average. What is the trend? Mark the answer in the "Trend" box. It is desirable for the last year to be higher than the average of the last five years.

2 EVALUATING MANAGEMENT

Company **JOHNSON & JOHNSON** **(JNJ)** 01/17/03

		1993	1994	1995	1996	1997	1998	1999	2000	2001	2002	LAST 5 YEAR AVG.	TREND UP	TREND DOWN
A	% Pre–tax Profit on Sales (Net Before Taxes ÷ Sales)	16.5	17.0	17.6	18.7	20.2	21.3	21.1	22.7	24.8	26.4	23.3	UP	
B	% Earned on Equity (E/S ÷ Book Value)	31.3	27.8	26.1	26.1	26.2	26.4	25.5	25.3	24.0	27.8	25.8	UP	

3 PRICE–EARNINGS HISTORY as an indicator of the future

This shows how stock prices have fluctuated with earnings and dividends. It is a building block for translating earnings into future stock prices.

PRESENT PRICE **54.790**　HIGH THIS YEAR **65.890**　LOW THIS YEAR **41.400**

	Year	A PRICE HIGH	B PRICE LOW	C Earnings Per Share	D Price Earnings Ratio HIGH A ÷ C	E Price Earnings Ratio LOW B ÷ C	F Dividend Per Share	G % Payout F ÷ C X 100	H % High Yield F ÷ B X 100
1	1998	44.9	31.7	1.34	33.6	23.7	0.485	36.3	1.5
2	1999	53.4	38.5	1.49	36.0	25.9	0.545	36.7	1.4
3	2000	53.0	33.1	1.71	31.0	19.4	0.620	36.3	1.9
4	2001	61.0	40.3	1.91	31.9	21.1	0.700	36.6	1.7
5	2002	65.9	41.4	2.25	29.3	18.4	0.800	35.6	1.9
6	TOTAL		185.0		161.8	108.5		181.5	
7	AVERAGE		37.0		32.4	21.7		36.3	
8	AVERAGE PRICE EARNINGS RATIO	27.1							
9	CURRENT PRICE EARNINGS RATIO				24.7				

Proj. P/E [21.84] Based on Next 4 qtr. EPS [2.51]　　Current P/E Based on Last 4 qtr. EPS [2.22]

4 EVALUATING RISK and REWARD over the next 5 years

Assuming one recession and one business boom every 5 years, calculations are made of how high and how low the stock might sell. The upside–downside ratio is th

A HIGH PRICE -- NEXT 5 YEARS
Avg. High P/E **32.4** 25.0 (3D7 as adj.) X Estimate High Earnings/Share **4.15** = Forecast High Price $ **103.8** (4A1)

B LOW PRICE -- NEXT 5 YEARS
(a) Avg. Low P/E **21.7** 18.0 (3E7 as adj.) X Estimated Low Earnings/Share **2.25** = $ **40.5**
(b) Avg. Low Price of Last 5 Years = **37.0** (3B7)
(c) Recent Severe Market Low Price = **40.3**
(d) Price Dividend Will Support Present Divd. = **0.840** = **43.5**　High Yield (H) **0.019**
Selected Estimate Low Price _____ = $ **40.5** (4B1)

C ZONING
103.8 (4A1) High Forecast Price Minus **40.5** (4B1) Low Forecast Price Equals **63.3** (C) Range. 1/3 of Range = **21.1** (4CD)
(4C2) Lower 1/3 = (4B1) **40.5** to **61.6** (Buy)
(4C3) Middle 1/3 = **61.6** to **82.7** (Maybe)
(4C4) Upper 1/3 = **82.7** to **103.8** (4A1) (Sell)
Present Market Price of **54.790** is in the **Buy** (4C5) Range

D UP–SIDE DOWN–SIDE RATIO (Potential Gain vs. Risk of Loss)
High Price (4A1) **103.8** Minus Present Price **54.790**
Present Price **54.790** Minus Low Price (4B1) **40.5** = **49.0** / **14.3** = **3.4** (4D) To 1

E PRICE TARGET (Note: This shows the potential market price appreciation over the next five years in simple interest terms.)
High Price (4A1) **103.8**
Present Market Price **54.790** = (**1.895**) X 100 = (**189.5**) – 100 = **89.5** (4E) % Appreciation

Relative Value: 91.1% Proj. Relative Value: 80.6%

5 5–YEAR POTENTIAL

This combines price appreciation with dividend yield to get an estimate of total return. It provides a standard for comparing inco

Note: Results are expressed as a simple rate; use the table below to convert to a compound rate.

A Present Full Year's Dividend $ **0.840**
Present Price of Stock $ **54.790** = **0.015** X 100 = **1.5** (5A) Present Yield or % Returned on Purchase Price

B AVERAGE YIELD OVER NEXT 5 YEARS
Avg. Earnings Per Share Next 5 Years **3.25** X Avg. % Payout (3G7) **36.3** = **118.0** = **2.2** % (5B)
Present Price $ **54.790**

C ESTIMATED AVERAGE ANNUAL RETURN OVER NEXT FIVE YEARS
5 Year Appreciation Potential (4E) **89.5** / 5 = **17.9** %
Average Yield (5B) = **2.2** %
Average Total Annual Return Over the Next 5 Years (5C) **20.1** %

Table to Convert from Simple to Compound Rates

Simple Rate: 2 4 6 8 10 12 14 16 18 20 22 24 26 28 30 32 34 36 38 40
2 4 6 8 10 12 14 16 18 20 22 24

Figure 21-01: Evaluating Management

What Do the Trends Tell You?

As you review the 10-year data compiled in Section 2, you should look for patterns. Are 2A and 2B fairly stable, increasing or declining? Or are the numbers all over the board? Good management attempts to control these key ratios, producing either stable patterns or slightly increasing trends.

As in Section 1 on Page 1, you may want to eliminate "abnormal" or "atypical" data (outliers) from your trend consideration in this section. The most recent five-year period is generally more important to you than the earlier five-year period. The recent past carries more weight in an investor's decision.

Pre-tax profit margins that are stable or increasing are positive indicators. Declining margins are "red flags" and should be studied to find out why. The same is true of return on equity. Decreasing pre-tax profits and the percent earned on equity may be indicators that increasing competition, rising labor and raw material costs or product quality problems are plaguing the company. You want to know what is going on.

Pre-tax profit margin and percent earned on equity trends should be compared with trends among other companies in the same industry. The industry data are available in both S&P and Value Line. If the trends in the company you are studying are unfavorable compared with the industry as a whole, you may be justified in terminating your study of that particular stock.

Examples of Section 2A and 2B for Johnson & Johnson are found on page 140.

SUMMARY

The objective of this chapter is to study two fundamental ratios that can evaluate management's ability to control costs and to produce appropriate returns on the funds stockholders have entrusted to them. The pre-tax profit margin and percent earned on equity ratios are critical in your evaluation of the management of the company you are studying.

KEY WORDS

PRE-TAX PROFIT ON SALES
PERCENT EARNED ON EQUITY
OUTLIERS
STABLE PATTERNS
INCREASING TRENDS

QUESTIONS

1. Fill in 2A & 2B using figures for the company you are studying.

   ■

2. What is your opinion of that company's management based on the data in 2A and 2B?

   ■

3. Explain why the pre-tax profit margins and percent earned on equity are used to evaluate management.

   ■

4. What types of patterns for pre-tax profit margins and percent earned on equity are indicators of good management?

   ■

5. Why should you obtain all your SSG data from the same information source?

Estimating Future Growth Rates

Chapter Goals—

After studying and reviewing this chapter, you will be able to:

- List some of the major questions to consider when estimating future sales and EPS growth rates for a company.

- Name a dozen other "qualitative factors" to consider when making the future growth rate estimates.

- Explain the guidelines for making reasonable growth rate projections.

- List four major precautions you should take when projecting future growth rates.

- Draw projection lines for sales and EPS growth.

Introduction

In Chapters 20 and 21, you learned how to estimate a company's historical growth rates for sales (revenues) and EPS and how to evaluate management by examining pre-tax profit margins and percent earned on equity. Historical growth rates and the two key ratios will be instrumental in the next step, estimating future growth rates for sales and EPS.

Estimating Future Growth Rates

You have learned to plot historical data and draw trend lines on the SSG graph. You now have a feel for a company's sales (revenues) and EPS performance over a period of years. You can actually visualize the sales and earnings trends. Using the pre-drawn percentage growth lines on the graph, you have also determined past growth rates for revenues and EPS. But now your judgment really comes into play! You need to form a picture of the company's future growth prospects. Remember, investors in common stocks are buying the future, not the past. Here are some of the questions you should ask yourself when you are trying to estimate future growth rates:

Is growth likely to continue in the future at the same rate as in the past?

Can a company growing at a very rapid rate (i.e., over 20%) sustain that rate in the future?

If pre-tax profit margins and return on equity percentages have been improving, should these be factored into the future growth rate of EPS?

How is Management Producing Growth?

- By introducing new products?
- By developing new uses for an old product?
- By developing variations of an established product?
- By regional expansion?
- By international expansion?
- By research and development on new products?
- By acquisition (of other companies)?

Understanding how management is producing growth will help you develop a good impression of how fast and how long growth may continue.

The answers to these questions come from research and from probing into the inner workings of the company and its industry. As companies get larger, it becomes more and more difficult to maintain very rapid growth rates. Thus, when you are looking to the future, it may be prudent to estimate a slowing down of growth rates.

Judgment Comes Into Play

It is wise to do research in the following areas before you estimate the future growth rates for EPS and sales for the company you are studying:

- Status of the National economy (the business cycle).

- How dependent is your company on the state of the overall economy?

- State of the industry your company is in.

- How will the state of the industry affect your company?

- Is that industry growing or is it more like the buggy whip and the ice box?

- The breadth of the company's products and services.

- Are they new, developing or mature?

- Is the company researching and developing new products?

- How successful has it been with new products in the past?

- Industry prospects.

- Luxury or "big ticket" products are the first to go in bad times.

- Necessity items are not cyclical.

- Government can quickly cancel defense orders.

- Debt ratio compared to other companies in the same industry.

- If there are variations in the percent of growth of sales and earnings and the reasons for them.

The Directors

- Are they mostly insiders or independents?

- What are their levels of experience?

The Management

- Are the managers responsible for the past track record?

- Is there new management? It usually takes new management two-three years to turn around a bad situation.

Percent of pre-tax profit (Section 2A).

Percent earned on equity (Section 2B).

Sales

- Are fads producing the sales? Fads may go away.

- Are increased sales due to mergers? Has the company participated in profitable mergers in the past?

Market

- What are the company's market shares for its products/services?

- Is the company a one-product company?

- Are new global markets coming into play?

- Is there or will there be stiff competition that could affect profit margins?

Other Conditions

- Are there any lawsuits that could affect the company?

- Is the company embroiled in labor disputes?

Read publications from Value Line and Standard & Poor's, annual reports (including footnotes), business magazines, and online services. Tune in to business and stock market oriented radio and television programs. Take advantage of all sources of evaluation and forecasting information.

Projection Lines for Revenues & EPS

Your projections are evaluations of a company's growth prospects for the next five years. They involve critical judgments. You should make the sales projection before the earnings projection because sales are the lifeblood of the company and earnings are derived from sales. Here are some guidelines to consider when you estimate future growth rates:

1. Err on the side of conservatism.

2. You should not project a growth rate over 20% and generally not over 15%. As a company grows, it becomes more difficult to maintain a growth rate over 20%.

3. Sales (revenues) are the source of earnings. Generally, you should not project that earnings per share will grow at a faster rate than past sales.

4. If the historical growth rate of earnings per share is less than the sales growth rate, project future earnings at the historical earnings rate or lower. It will be risky to estimate an improvement in earnings growth.

5. The most recent five-year figures are much more important than the earlier five-year figures

6. The five-year projection line is drawn from the last data point (on the bold line) out to the right margin of the graph.

   If there was a large aberration (variance) at the last data point, it will then be best to use a projected estimation from another source such as Value Line.

7. When the projection lines have been drawn, the estimated five-year future sales and EPS figures are determined by where the projection line crosses the right hand margin. The dollar amounts are determined by the numerical values of the horizontal lines that run across the page.

8. Record the estimated past growth rate and the estimated future growth rate for both sales and earnings per share at the bottom of Page 1 of the Stock Selection Guide.

   If you encounter a situation where earnings per share are temporarily

growing at a faster rate than sales, you might want to consider the following possible reasons:

- Company buying back stock so that there are fewer shares outstanding.
- Company getting "lean and mean," downsizing by laying off personnel.
- Sale of assets, such as plants and other facilities.

CAUTION FLAG!
Be Careful About...

1. Projecting sales higher in future than in the past without clear knowledge of a major development.

2. Projecting sales or earnings over 20% or even over 15%.

3. Projecting earnings growth rates higher than sales.

4. Projecting earnings higher than they have been in the past unless you have strong reason to believe that pre-tax profit margins will increase.

Drawing EPS & Sales Projection Lines

After you have considered all the information and you have estimated five-year earnings and sales growth rate percentages, you are ready to draw the projection lines. Normally, trend lines are not used as projection lines. Here's how you proceed:

1. Using your information and the guidelines above, you estimate a future growth rate for the company. Measure down the bold 10-year line from the last earnings and sales data points to the pre-drawn guideline for the percentage you have chosen.

2. On the right margin, measure up that same distance from your growth percentage guide line. Mark that point.

3. Draw a line from the last data point (on the bold line) to this mark. This is your projection line.

Five-Year Dollar Projections

By observing where your projection line intersects the right margin line (five years in the future) and by noting the numerical value of the nearest horizontal line, you can assign dollar amounts to projected sales and earnings in five years.

An example of Johnson & Johnson projections follows on Page 148.

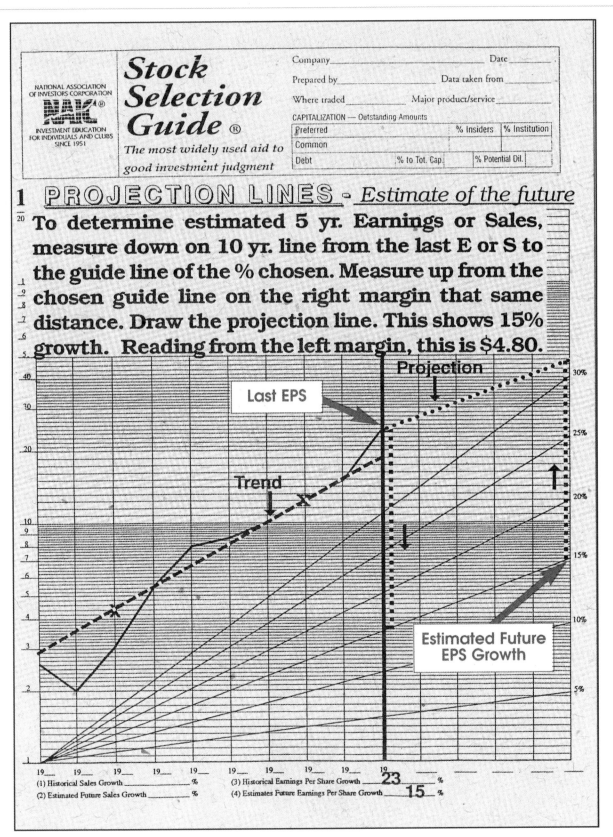

Figure 22-01: Projection Lines

Stock Selection Guide ®

The most widely used aid to good investment judgment

Company	**JOHNSON & JOHNSON**	Date	**01/17/03**
Prepared by	**NAIC**	Data taken from	**Value Line**
Where traded	**NYSE**	Major product/service	**Pharmaceuticals**

CAPITALIZATION --- Outstanding Amounts   Reference **pg. 213**

Preferred ($M)	**0.0**	% Insiders	% Institution	
Common (M Shares)	**2,970.6**	**0.2**	**61.9**	
Debt ($M)	**2,102.0**	% to Tot.Cap. **9.0**	% Potential Dil.	**None**

1   VISUAL ANALYSIS of Sales, Earnings and Price   JNJ

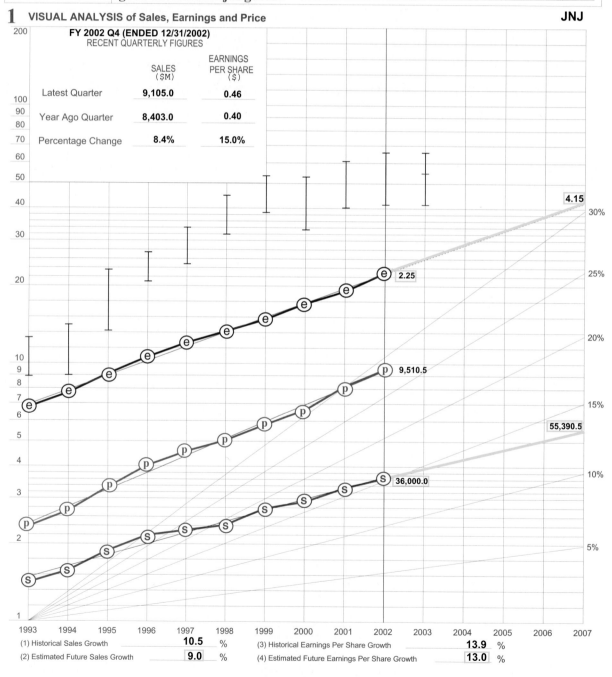

FY 2002 Q4 (ENDED 12/31/2002)
RECENT QUARTERLY FIGURES

	SALES ($M)	EARNINGS PER SHARE ($)
Latest Quarter	9,105.0	0.46
Year Ago Quarter	8,403.0	0.40
Percentage Change	8.4%	15.0%

(1) Historical Sales Growth **10.5** %

(2) Estimated Future Sales Growth **9.0** %

(3) Historical Earnings Per Share Growth **13.9** %

(4) Estimated Future Earnings Per Share Growth **13.0** %

Figure 22-02: Johnson & Johnson Projections

Evaluating Growth Projections

Now, armed with our projected growth rates for revenues and EPS, let's step back and analyze what we have. Does the company meet our target growth rates for the size of this company? Should the study be continued? Some evaluation questions:

1. Do the company's projected sales and earnings meet your target growth rates?

2. Are earnings per share growing at a rate that is faster, slower or about the same as sales?

3. Is the stock volatile?

4. Has the yearly price trend of the stock been similar to the growth rate of EPS? How has this growth been produced?

5. Can the future growth of sales, earnings and prices be easily established? If growth has been steady over at least the last five years, it is reasonable to expect steady growth in the future.

6. Were any extraordinary items included in the earnings?

7. Should the study be discontinued or completed?

Make the decision based on your own judgment. If your research indicates that future EPS growth might be disappointing, you can end the study right here and begin searching for another stock to study!

KEY WORDS

GUIDELINES
CAUTION FLAG
CONSERVATISM
HISTORICAL GROWTH RATE
FUTURE GROWTH RATE
PROJECTION LINE

SUMMARY

Estimating future growth of sales and earnings for a company is a pivotal activity. You take the historical data into account, but you also weigh in with your own judgment. Ideally, sales and earnings will continue to grow at the same rate as in the past, but you have to decide whether these growth rates appear to be sustainable and whether there are any new conditions that would cause you to modify your projection. It is your money and your call.

QUESTIONS & PROJECTS

1. State some important criteria to be considered before making projections.

   ■

2. Explain why sales projections are made before earnings.

   ■

3. Name the four things you have to be careful about when you are making the projections.

   ■

4. What is a reasonable growth rate projection for sales for the stock you are studying?

   ■

5. What is a reasonable growth rate projection for earnings per share for the stock you are studying?

   ■

6. Note these estimated future growth rate percentages on lines 2 and 4 at the bottom of the SSG graph.

   ■

7. Draw projection lines based on these growth rates on your graph.

Price-Earnings History

Chapter Goals–

After studying and reviewing this chapter, you will be able to:

• Understand the significance of P/E ratios.

• Calculate the high and low P/E for any given year.

• Determine the average five-year P/E.

• Understand the term "payout."

• Compute the percentage of payout.

• Understand what "yield" means.

• Determine the percentage of high yield during the last five years.

• Calculate the current P/E

Introduction

After completing Sections 1 and 2 of the SSG, you now have a "go" or "no-go" signal for the company you are studying. In other words, you have a pretty good idea whether that company has the kind of growth potential you want. If you are not satisfied with its growth prospects, it is time to drop the company and look for another candidate. If you are satisfied, then the big question is–what should I be willing to pay (common stock price) for that future growth? In this chapter, using Section 3 of the SSG, you will assemble some of the information needed to make that decision. An example Section 3 for Johnson & Johnson is found on Page 154.

Filling in Section 3 of the SSG

Using the stock table of your newspaper or an online source, fill in the information called for at the top of this section: the stock's most recent price, its high price for the current year (last 52 weeks) and its low price for the current year. Then, begin filling in the Price-Earnings Table. Enter the most recent five years (the most recent five years in Part 1 of your SSG) and list the following data from Value Line in columns A, B, C and F: (A) the high and (B) low common stock prices, (C) earnings per share and (F) dividends per share for those five years.

Price Earnings Ratios (P/E) – Columns D & E

The price/earnings ratio (P/E) is a way of measuring and comparing the value of stocks. It is a gauge for judging what you are getting for your money when you buy a certain stock.

The symbol P/E means what it says: the price of a share divided by earnings per share. You may sometimes find it written PE without the division sign. "Multiple" or "times" are other terms for P/E. You may hear that a stock is selling at a "multiple of 15." Or that it is selling at "15 times." In other words, investors are paying $15 for $1 worth of earnings. The stock's P/E is 15.

P/E represents how people feel about a certain stock. If they think the company has strong growth potential, they will pay more for the stock, resulting in a higher P/E. A high P/E reflects expectations of rapid growth; a low P/E reflects expectations of sluggish growth. A low P/E may be a warning sign that a stock probably will not meet your growth objectives. But when you find a company where the vital signs are strong (sales, earnings, profit margins, etc.), you want to get the stock at the lowest P/E possible.

Sometimes the entire stock market is down (a bear market), high quality stocks included. At these times, you can buy stock in a good company at a low P/E. The stock market is sensitive to all sorts of political and economic conditions–wars and other national catastrophes, interest and inflation rates, unemployment levels, etc.

Many growth companies are less vulnerable to the cyclical ups and downs of the general economy. Their stocks will display consistent above-average growth, and generally, they will command higher P/E's than slower-growth or cyclical companies.

P/E ratios can become inflated in bull markets when people are betting on future prices and future earnings and are willing to pay stock prices that are not justified by current earnings. During the late 1990s Internet stock prices went into the stratosphere and lost touch with earnings. The collapse of stock prices that followed–and the number of people who lost their shirts–was a harsh reminder of the importance of paying attention to P/E ratios.

Your next step is to fill in the high and low P/E ratios for your stock for all five years. If you are using Standard & Poor's, the calculations have been done for you. If your information source is Value Line, you need to do the simple arithmetic called for at the top of columns D and E: To compute the high P/E, you simply divide the high price (column A) by EPS (column C) and record the ratio in column D. It is interesting to note the annual P/E ranges (high to low). The highs and lows indicate how much or how little investors were valuing the stock throughout the year.

% Payout and % High Yield–Columns G & H

The term "payout" (column G) refers to the percentage of net income that the company pays out to shareholders in the form of cash dividends (F/C). Remember, growth companies typically do not pay out a large percentage of their net earnings. They prefer to reinvest the profits to help the business continue growing.

Column H entitled "% High Yield" represents the dividend per share (column F) divided by the lowest price a stock reaches in a specific year (column B). All of the calculations in columns G and H are multiplied by 100 to express them as percentages.

Many small companies do not pay a dividend, but retain their earnings to support company growth. If the fundamentals are good, this is highly desirable. A well-managed company that is growing fast will need to invest in new activities and new facilities. The reward to stockholders will be a growth in the price of the stock they own (capital appreciation).

A mature company tends to pay higher dividends. As it gets larger and larger, its growth rate slows, and more of the earnings can be paid out in dividends.

Computing the Averages

With the data filled in on lines 1 through 5 for columns A-H, it is time to compute some averages. You start with column B, adding the five years of low prices, finding the sum, then dividing by 5 to reach the average low price. You record it in box 7-B. Then you calculate the averages for columns D, E and G the same way.

Note: An unusually high or low P/E should be considered an outlier and excluded from the averaging. Just remember to divide by 4 instead of 5. A P/E dropped from the high or low column does not require dropping the corresponding number from the other column.

The next step is to compute the average price earnings ratio for the past five years. You simply add box 7-D (average high P/E) and box 7-E (average low P/E) and divide by 2. Enter this figure, the average P/E, into box 8. **Note**: Neither S&P nor Value Line provides a five-year average P/E.

Finally, we turn to box 9, the current P/E. You can calculate this ratio by dividing the most recent price of the stock, as recorded at the top of Section 3, by the total of the earnings per share for the most recent four quarters. Or you can simply use the P/E you find in the same newspaper from which you have taken the stock price. Sometimes, you will see this P/E calculated on the estimated EPS for the next 12 months. This is called the projected P/E (PPE).

What Does It All Mean?

Section 3 is entirely historical information. By looking at these price and earnings trends and averages, you have important new information about the stock you are studying.

Price Trends: In columns A and B, you have an overview of common stock price trends for the past five years. Ideally, you want to see both the high and the low prices trending higher from year to year. This indicates a growing company. If the common stock price has been relatively stagnant, you have to ask why—and what it will take to change this pattern.

Price Volatility: Look at the differences between high and low prices for each year. If stock A had a high of $50 and a low of $45 and stock B had a high of $50 and a low of $20, what would you say about the volatility of these two stocks? Look for patterns in the range of high and low stock prices. Remember, the price patterns are nice to know, but the NAIC approach is grounded in the underlying fundamentals of the company (growth in revenues and earnings). If the fundamentals are solid, that will be reflected in the price of the stock!

Earnings per Share: Column C is another record of the company's EPS. (There is also one on the first page of the SSG.) This is crucial information. Your goal is to find companies that show consistent, sustainable growth in EPS.

P/E Ratios: The high and low P/E ratios should be reviewed for trends. It is considered a good sign when the P/Es have increased at a steady rate or remained fairly stable. If the P/E ratios have been going down steadily, it is not a healthy signal.

Dividends: The dividend per share column has no significance for many smaller, growth companies that pay no dividends. The payout ratio tells you whether a company's management is growth minded. Companies that pay out a large percentage of net earnings (say, over 50%) are considered "income stocks" with high dividend yields. Growth stocks tend to have minimal dividend payouts.

The "% high yield" calculation will be used in estimating a low price in the next chapter.

2 EVALUATING MANAGEMENT

Company **JOHNSON & JOHNSON** **(JNJ)** 01/17/03

		1993	1994	1995	1996	1997	1998	1999	2000	2001	2002	LAST 5 YEAR AVG.	TREND UP	TREND DOWN
A	% Pre-tax Profit on Sales (Net Before Taxes ÷ Sales)	16.5	17.0	17.6	18.7	20.2	21.3	21.1	22.7	24.8	26.4	23.3	UP	
B	% Earned on Equity (E/S ÷ Book Value)	31.3	27.8	26.1	26.1	26.2	26.4	25.5	25.3	24.0	27.8	25.8	UP	

3 PRICE–EARNINGS HISTORY as an indicator of the future

This shows how stock prices have fluctuated with earnings and dividends. It is a building block for translating earnings into future stock prices.

PRESENT PRICE **54.790** HIGH THIS YEAR **65.890** LOW THIS YEAR **41.400**

	Year	A HIGH	B LOW	C Earnings Per Share	D HIGH A ÷ C	E LOW B ÷ C	F Dividend Per Share	G % Payout F ÷ C X 100	H % High Yield F ÷ B X 100
1	1998	44.9	31.7	1.34	33.6	23.7	0.485	36.3	1.5
2	1999	53.4	38.5	1.49	36.0	25.9	0.545	36.7	1.4
3	2000	53.0	33.1	1.71	31.0	19.4	0.620	36.3	1.9
4	2001	61.0	40.3	1.91	31.9	21.1	0.700	36.6	1.7
5	2002	65.9	41.4	2.25	29.3	18.4	0.800	35.6	1.9
6	TOTAL		185.0		161.8	108.5		181.5	
7	AVERAGE		37.0		32.4	21.7		36.3	
8	AVERAGE PRICE EARNINGS RATIO	27.1		9 CURRENT PRICE EARNINGS RATIO		24.7			

Proj. P/E [21.84] Based on Next 4 qtr. EPS [2.51]   Current P/E Based on Last 4 qtr. EPS [2.22]

4 EVALUATING RISK and REWARD over the next 5 years

Assuming one recession and one business boom every 5 years, calculations are made of how high and how low the stock might sell. The upside–downside ratio is the key t

A HIGH PRICE -- NEXT 5 YEARS
Avg. High P/E **32.4** **25.0** X Estimate High Earnings/Share **4.15** = Forecast High Price $ **103.8**
(3D7 as adj.) (4A1)

B LOW PRICE -- NEXT 5 YEARS
(a) Avg. Low P/E **21.7** **18.0** X Estimated Low Earnings/Share **2.25** = $ **40.5**
(3E7 as adj.)
(b) Avg. Low Price of Last 5 Years = **37.0**
(3B7)
(c) Recent Severe Market Low Price = **40.3**
(d) Price Dividend Will Support Present Divd. = **0.840** = **43.5**
High Yield (H) **0.019**
Selected Estimate Low Price = $ **40.5**
(4B1)

C ZONING
103.8 High Forecast Price Minus **40.5** Low Forecast Price Equals **63.3** Range. 1/3 of Range = **21.1**
(4A1) (4B1) (C) (4CD)

(4C2) Lower 1/3 = (4B1) **40.5** to **61.6** (Buy)
(4C3) Middle 1/3 = **61.6** to **82.7** (Maybe)
(4C4) Upper 1/3 = **82.7** to **103.8** (4A1) (Sell)

Present Market Price of **54.790** is in the **Buy** Range
(4C5)

D UP–SIDE DOWN–SIDE RATIO (Potential Gain vs. Risk of Loss)
High Price (4A1) **103.8** Minus Present Price **54.790**
Present Price **54.790** Minus Low Price (4B1) **40.5** = $\frac{49.0}{14.3}$ = **3.4** To 1
(4D)

E PRICE TARGET (Note: This shows the potential market price appreciation over the next five years in simple interest terms.)
High Price (4A1) **103.8**
Present Market Price **54.790** = (**1.895**) X 100 = (**189.5**) – 100 = **89.5** % Appreciation
(4E)

Relative Value: 91.1% Proj. Relative Value: 80.6%

5 5–YEAR POTENTIAL

This combines price appreciation with dividend yield to get an estimate of total return. It provides a standard for comparing income and

Note: Results are expressed as a simple rate; use the table below to convert to a compound rate.

A Present Full Year's Dividend $ 0.840
Present Price of Stock $ **54.790** = **0.015** X 100 = **1.5** Present Yield or % Returned on Purchase Price
(5A)

B AVERAGE YIELD OVER NEXT 5 YEARS
Avg. Earnings Per Share Next 5 Years **3.25** X Avg. % Payout (3G7) **36.3** = **118.0** = **2.2** %
Present Price $ **54.790** (5B)

C ESTIMATED AVERAGE ANNUAL RETURN OVER NEXT FIVE YEARS
5 Year Appreciation Potential (4E) **89.5**
$\frac{}{5}$ **17.9** %

Table to Convert from Simple to Compound Rates

Average Yield (5B) **2.2** %   Simple Rate 2 4 6 8 10 12 14 16 18 20 22 24 26 28 30 32 34 36 38 40
Average Total Annual Return Over the Next 5 Years (5C) **20.1** %   2 4 6 8 10 12 14 16 18 20 22 24

Figure 23-01: Price Earnings History

SUMMARY

Section 3 shows the relationships between price, earnings and dividends. The price earnings ratio (P/E) is a measure of the value of the stock. Payout refers to the percent of earnings paid to the shareholders. The dollar amount paid out is the dividend, and the dividend as a ratio to the price is called the yield.

KEY WORDS

PRICE EARNINGS RATIO
MULTIPLE
TIMES
PAYOUT
HIGH YIELD
CURRENT P/E RATIO
AVERAGE HISTORICAL P/E
OUTLIERS

QUESTIONS & PROJECTS

1. Complete Section 3 for the company you are studying.

    ■

2. Explain the importance of P/E ratios.
    What does a high P/E indicate?
    What does a low P/E indicate?

    ■

3. What other two terms are sometimes used for P/E?

    ■

4. Define the term "payout."

    ■

5. Why do some small companies not pay a dividend? Is that necessarily bad for a stockholder?

    ■

6. What kind of pattern should you look for in P/Es?
    Should you ever shop for a low P/E?

Evaluating Risk & Reward

Chapter Goals—

After studying and reviewing this chapter, you will be able to:

- *Forecast the high price the company's stock might reach in the next five years.*

- *Use four different methods of estimating the low price the stock might reach in the next five years.*

- *Determine the most likely low price forecast for the next five years.*

- *Establish BUY, MAYBE and SELL price ranges.*

- *Explain the formula for finding the upside/downside ratio.*

- *Use the upside/downside ratio to achieve a desirable relationship between potential reward and risk.*

- *Estimate future price appreciation.*

Introduction

Let's look at what you have accomplished so far. You have created a visual analysis of trends for a company's revenues, earnings per share and common stock price, and you have drawn future projections. You have evaluated the company's management based on pre-tax profit margins and return on equity ratios. In Section 3, you examined the company's five-year price-earnings history as an indicator of the future. All of this information leads to Section 4, which will help you decide whether the stock in question is attractive for purchase or appears overvalued and should not be purchased. In this chapter, you will learn about estimating high and low prices for the next five years. Using these numbers you will establish buy, sell and maybe price ranges, and you will learn how to achieve a positive balance between reward and risk in making a stock-purchasing decision.

Section 4A–Forecasting a High Price

The first step in Section 4 is to estimate the high price the stock might reach within the next five years. You compute this price by multiplying the average high price P/E (box 7D from Section 3) by the estimated high earnings per share.

This estimated high EPS is generated from the EPS projection line you drew on the graph on Page 1. You take your figure from where the EPS projection line intersects the line for year five (the last line on the right).

There is room for your own judgment when estimating the high price for the next five years. You do not have to stick rigidly to the average high P/E from the past, but you may choose a P/E which feels more comfortable and which you can justify.

Remember that a stock's P/E ratio not only reflects how investors are responding to a company's past performance and growth rate, but also their expectations for the future. If the growth rate of a company you are studying is slowing

down, you should expect the P/E ratio to decline too, and you may want to base your high price projection on a number somewhat lower than the average high P/E. In our Johnson & Johnson example that is exactly what we did.

You also need to be aware of the fact that P/E ratios rose to unprecedented high levels in the speculative investment climate of the late 1990s. The average stock's P/E ratio is now in the 20s and JNJ's average high P/E of 32 is above that average. In light of these facts, we very conservatively lowered our estimated high P/E of JNJ to 25.

Section 4B–Forecasting a Low Price

Next, we want to select our "downside risk" or low price for the next five years. This section offers four methods for estimating how low the price might drop within the next five years.

The Four Methods

1. **Line 4B(a)** computes low price per share in the next five years by multiplying the average low P/E (7B in Section 3) by the estimated low earnings per share. Because you are studying the stock of a growth company, the most recent

year's earnings (5C) are used for the low earnings per share estimate. This EPS should be a low figure relative to the projected EPS over the next five years. Again, you should apply your judgment to selecting the representative low P/E ratio from column E. This method is appropriate for companies that display consistent growth.

2. **Line 4B(b)** simply accepts the average low stock price for the past five years (7B in Section 3) as

the estimated low price for the next five. This method is more appropriate for estimating the future low price for cyclical companies where the price movement is dictated more by general economic conditions than by growth in the company. These include companies in industries such as automobiles, chemicals and paper.

3. **Line 4B(c)** asks for the "Recent Severe Market Low Price" from the Section 3 chart. Note that the severe market low price is not necessarily the lowest price in Section 3, column B. A severe market is a bear market, a significant downturn in

the overall stock market. Severe market lows are noted in grayed columns within the graph at the top of the Value Line sheets. Standard and Poor's does not provide a severe market indicator.

The severe market low is used is to suggest how far a price might fall when the overall stock market is low. Such a time often provides a buying opportunity for fundamentally strong stocks. You must use your judgment in selecting a low price for this line. Method (c), like (b), is a better guide for selecting the low price for cyclical companies, where price movement is dictated more by general economic conditions than by growth in the company.

4. **Line 4B(d)** asks for the "Price (the) Dividend Will Support." The formula to compute this number is provided: You divide the present dividend of the company by the highest number in the High Yield column (H). If the dividend is paid quarterly, multiply the last quarter's dividend (#5 section of Value Line) by 4 to get the present annual dividend.

This method is based on the fact that companies rarely decrease their dividend. Management likes to boast that they have maintained or raised their dividend for many years. This dividend yield acts as a buffer when a company's stock may be declining. There is a point where the dividend will attract investors and the dividend will support that particular price level. This approach to selecting a low price has more relevance for income (dividend) producing stocks than growth stocks. You will find income stocks in industries such as utilities and banking and in mature, large companies.

Using Your Judgment

From what you have learned by examining these four methods, you must select a low price for the next five years. You know that the four methods are suited to different types of companies. Still, there are times when good judgment suggests a price somewhere in the middle of those prices. The low price of the last 52 weeks should be noted. If, for instance, the

company is a good growth company where you would normally choose 4B(a), but the 52-week low price or current price is very close to the 4B(a) price, you may need a lower estimate. Certainly, you can never use a low price that is higher than the present price of the stock.

You should never just average the four methods. Doing so has no meaning. Many investors frequently select a low price that is around 10% to 25% below the current price of the stock under study–to acknowledge the possibility of a general stock market correction. You should use your own best judgment in estimating a low price (or downside risk) for the next five years.

Zoning–Section 4C

Our next step is to establish three price zones between the high and low prices you have forecast in 4A and 4B. From this, we will arrive at BUY, MAYBE (or HOLD) and SELL indicators.

First, subtract the low forecast price from the high forecast price and divide by 3. Put this number in box 4CD.

- **BUY range =**
  up to low forecast
  price + number in 4CD.

- **SELL range =**
  down to high forecast price
  – number in 4CD.

- **MAYBE/HOLD =**
  range between
  BUY and SELL numbers.

Johnson & Johnson's Calculations for Section 4C

High forecast price	$103.8
Low forecast price	− $ 40.5
	= $ 63.3
	$63.3 / 3 = $ 21.1

BUY: $40.5 + $21.1 = $61.6
a price below $61.6

SELL: $103.8 − $21.1 = $82.7
a price above $82.7

MAYBE: a price between
$61.6 and $82.7

The last line in Section 4C requires you to write in the present market price of the stock under study and indicate which zone it falls into (BUY, MAYBE or SELL).

Note: Many NAIC investors use a 25-50-25% Buy, Maybe, Sell range, as found in the *Investor's Toolkit* SSG software.

Upside/Downside Ratio– Section 4D

If your high and low price forecasts are reasonably accurate, the upside/downside ratio will help you get a feel for whether the risks are worth taking. Ideally, you want to buy a significantly higher reward potential than level of risk. The upside/downside ratio attempts to estimate this relationship. The NAIC recommends looking for at least a 3 to 1 upside/ downside ratio to make your decision a prudent one. After all, you want to buy towards the lower end of the BUY range, not the high end (buy low, sell high). Let's see how the ratio works:

Johnson & Johnson Calculations for Section 4D

$$\frac{\text{high price} - \text{present price}}{\text{present price} - \text{low price}}$$

$$= \text{upside/downside ratio}$$

Step 1. High forecast price minus present price = numerator

Step 2. Present price minus selected low price = denominator

Step 3. Division gives the estimated ratio of reward to risk

High forecast price =	$103.8
Present price =	$ 54.8
Low forecast price =	$ 40.5

Step 1. $103.8 − $54.8 = $49.0
Step 2. $ 54.8 − $40.5 = $14.3
Step 3. $ 49.0 / $14.3 = 3.4 to 1

Johnson & Johnson has the recommended 3 to 1 upside/downside ratio. The stock price is in the upper half of the buy zone.

Abnormally High Upside/Downside Ratios

You should be careful if you have an abnormally high upside/downside ratio. Ratios of 10 to 1 or higher should be questioned:

- Re-check the high and low forecast prices for accuracy.

- Have you used a sufficiently conservative estimated low price? The estimated low price greatly affects the upside/downside ratio.

An abnormally high upside/downside ratio indicates that the stock is currently selling at or near its projected low for the next five years.

The upside/downside ratio is an indicator of the attractiveness of an investment. It is another tool for making a rational decision. Be honest with yourself and never force estimated high or low prices by manipulating the figures. They must be reasonable.

Section 4E—Price Appreciation

This section provides a way of using your estimated high price to determine whether the stock you are studying should double in price (or grow by

100%) in the next five years. Here's the formula:

$$\frac{estimated\ high\ price}{present\ price \times 100 - 100} = potential\ five\text{-}year\ appreciation$$

The target should be double (100% appreciation) the present stock price. Thus, the answer to Section 4E should be fairly close to 100% or better. Note: If there is a dividend, the average annual dividend may be added to the price appreciation to estimate the total return. This is discussed in the next chapter.

Johnson & Johnson Calculations for Section 4E

Estimated high price	**$103.8**
Present price	**$ 54.8**
Step 1. $103.8 / 54.8 =	1.895
Step 2. 1.895 x 100 =	189.5
Step 3. 189.5 − 100 =	89.5%
	appreciation in price

Johnson & Johnson's potential price appreciation is very close to the NAIC goal of doubling within the next five years. We will see in the next section that the dividend income component of annual return will put JNJ "over the top." Of course, other criteria will also be taken into consideration. A BUY is not based only on one portion of the study. All factors must be considered.

2 EVALUATING MANAGEMENT

Company **JOHNSON & JOHNSON** **(JNJ)** 01/17/03

		1993	1994	1995	1996	1997	1998	1999	2000	2001	2002	LAST 5 YEAR AVG.	TREND UP	TREND DOWN
A	% Pre–tax Profit on Sales (Net Before Taxes ÷ Sales)	16.5	17.0	17.6	18.7	20.2	21.3	21.1	22.7	24.8	26.4	23.3	UP	
B	% Earned on Equity (E/S ÷ Book Value)	31.3	27.8	26.1	26.1	26.2	26.4	25.5	25.3	24.0	27.8	25.8	UP	

3 PRICE–EARNINGS HISTORY as an indicator of the future

This shows how stock prices have fluctuated with earnings and dividends. It is a building block for translating earnings into future stock prices.

PRESENT PRICE **54.790** HIGH THIS YEAR **65.890** LOW THIS YEAR **41.400**

	Year	A PRICE HIGH	B PRICE LOW	C Earnings Per Share	D Price Earnings Ratio HIGH A ÷ C	E Price Earnings Ratio LOW B ÷ C	F Dividend Per Share	G % Payout F ÷ C X 100	H % High Yield F ÷ B X 100
1	1998	44.9	31.7	1.34	33.6	23.7	0.485	36.3	1.5
2	1999	53.4	38.5	1.49	36.0	25.9	0.545	36.7	1.4
3	2000	53.0	33.1	1.71	31.0	19.4	0.620	36.3	1.9
4	2001	61.0	40.3	1.91	31.9	21.1	0.700	36.6	1.7
5	2002	65.9	41.4	2.25	29.3	18.4	0.800	35.6	1.9
6	TOTAL		185.0		161.8	108.5		181.5	
7	AVERAGE		37.0		32.4	21.7		36.3	
8	AVERAGE PRICE EARNINGS RATIO		27.1						
9	CURRENT PRICE EARNINGS RATIO						24.7		

4 EVALUATING RISK and REWARD over the next 5 years

Proj. P/E [21.84] Based on Next 4 qtr. EPS [2.51]   Current P/E Based on Last 4 qtr. EPS [2.22]

Assuming one recession and one business boom every 5 years, calculations are made of how high and how low the stock might sell. The upside–downside ratio is the key to

A HIGH PRICE -- NEXT 5 YEARS
Avg. High P/E **32.4** **25.0** (3D7 as adj.) X Estimate High Earnings/Share **4.15** = Forecast High Price $ **103.8** (4A1)

B LOW PRICE -- NEXT 5 YEARS
(a) Avg. Low P/E **21.7** **18.0** (3E7 as adj.) X Estimated Low Earnings/Share **2.25** = $ **40.5**
(b) Avg. Low Price of Last 5 Years = **37.0** (3B7)
(c) Recent Severe Market Low Price = **40.3**
(d) Price Dividend Will Support Present Divd. = **0.840** = **43.5**
    High Yield (H) **0.019**
Selected Estimate Low Price = $ **40.5** (4B1)

C ZONING
103.8 (4A1) High Forecast Price Minus **40.5** (4B1) Low Forecast Price Equals **63.3** (C) Range. 1/3 of Range = **21.1** (4CD)

(4C2) Lower 1/3 = (4B1) **40.5** to **61.6** (Buy)
(4C3) Middle 1/3 = **61.6** to **82.7** (Maybe)
(4C4) Upper 1/3 = **82.7** to **103.8** (4A1) (Sell)

Present Market Price of **54.790** is in the **Buy** (4C5) Range

D UP-SIDE DOWN-SIDE RATIO (Potential Gain vs. Risk of Loss)
High Price (4A1) **103.8** Minus Present Price **54.790**
Present Price **54.790** Minus Low Price (4B1) **40.5** = **49.0 / 14.3** = **3.4** (4D) To 1

E PRICE TARGET (Note: This shows the potential market price appreciation over the next five years in simple interest terms.)
High Price (4A1) **103.8**
Present Market Price **54.790** = (**1.895**) X 100 = (**189.5**) – 100 = **89.5** (4E) % Appreciation

Relative Value: 91.1%   Proj. Relative Value: 80.6%

5 5-YEAR POTENTIAL

This combines price appreciation with dividend yield to get an estimate of total return. It provides a standard for comparing income and

Note: Results are expressed as a simple rate; use the table below to convert to a compound rate.

A Present Full Year's Dividend $ **0.840**
Present Price of Stock $ **54.790** = **0.015** X 100 = **1.5** (5A) Present Yield or % Returned on Purchase Price

B AVERAGE YIELD OVER NEXT 5 YEARS
Avg. Earnings Per Share Next 5 Years **3.25** X Avg. % Payout (3G7) **36.3** = **118.0** = **2.2** (5B) %
Present Price $ **54.790**

C ESTIMATED AVERAGE ANNUAL RETURN OVER NEXT FIVE YEARS
5 Year Appreciation Potential (4E) **89.5** / 5 = **17.9** %
Average Yield (5B) = **2.2** %
Average Total Annual Return Over the Next 5 Years (5C) = **20.1** %

Table to Convert from Simple to Compound Rates

Simple Rate: 2 4 6 8 10 12 14 16 18 20 22 24 26 28 30 32 34 36 38 40
2 4 6 8 10 12 14 16 18 20 22 24

Figure 24-01: Risk and Reward

EVALUATING RISK & REWARD

SUMMARY

The estimated high price in the next five years is determined by multiplying the average high P/E (after adjustments) by the estimated high earnings per share. There are four ways to estimate where the low price may fall within the next five years. There may be situations which call for choosing a low price somewhere in the middle of the calculated low prices. BUY, MAYBE and SELL ranges are determined by dividing the difference between the estimated high and low prices into thirds. When you buy a stock, it is important to estimate the risk/reward ratio. If you think a stock you own has reached its potential, do a new set of SSG calculations before selling it. Remember your goal: the stock price (plus dividend yield) should double in the next five years.

KEY WORDS

ZONING
ABNORMALLY HIGH
TARGET PRICE
UPSIDE/DOWNSIDE RATIO
HIGH PRICE–NEXT FIVE YEARS
LOW PRICE–NEXT FIVE YEARS
CONSISTENT GROWTH
CYCLICAL
INCOME PRODUCING
BUY
MAYBE
SELL
PRICE APPRECIATION

QUESTIONS & PROJECTS

1. On your SSG, calculate the estimated high price asked for on 4A.

2. For the stock you are studying, calculate the four methods for estimating a possible low price asked for in 4B(a), 4B(b), 4B(c) and 4B(d).

3. Explain when it is most appropriate to use each of the four methods for estimating future low price.

4. What situations may cause you to choose a price other than those shown by the four low prices calculated?

5. Choose an estimated low price for your study.

6. Explain how to find the BUY, MAYBE and SELL zones.

7. Calculate the BUY, MAYBE and SELL zones on your stock study.

8. Explain the upside/downside ratio.

9. Calculate the upside/downside ratio for the stock you are studying and complete Section 4D.

10. Complete Section 4E for the stock you are studying.

11. State whether your stock has an upside/downside ratio that meets the suggested NAIC goal.

163

The Five-Year Potential

Chapter Goals—

After studying and reviewing this chapter, you will be able to:

• Explain the dividend policy.

• Find the percentage of return on the present purchase price.

• Know what figure to use for the full year's dividend.

• Find the average yield over the next five years.

• Find the estimated annual return (arithmetic) over the next five years.

Introduction

The last step in completing the SSG is Section 5, entitled "Five-Year Potential." In this section, you will estimate the annual total return for the stock you are studying. Remember that total return includes your return from the stock's price appreciation and dividend yield. This calculation is not intended to be precise, but rather an average (ballpark) figure. This number is not a compound growth rate. It is a simple interest growth rate and must be 20% to double in five years.

Dividend Policy for Companies

Management's dividend policy indicates the company's growth stage. A new company may not pay a dividend. A developing company may pay a small dividend. A mature company typically pays a larger dividend. The smaller the company the greater the need to retain earnings to help the company to grow.

Calculating Present (Current) Yield—Section 5A

Section 5A asks you to calculate the present yield (also called current yield) of your stock. Here's the formula:

$$\frac{Present\ full\ year\ dividend}{Present\ market\ price\ of\ stock} \times 100 = Present\ yield$$

Present Yield–Johnson & Johnson

Current annual dividend
per share   = $ .84
Present stock price
per share   = $54.79
.84 / 54.79   =   .015
.015 x 100   =   1.5%

Note: Remember to multiply a quarterly dividend by 4 to determine the annual dividend before doing the above calculations for any stock you are studying.

The present or current yield of a common stock basically tells you how much of your annual return is from dividend income. You should be aware of this information, but remember that this figure is only your "present yield" and does not reflect future (potential) dividend increases. Section 5B estimates an average yield over the next five years.

Average Yield over Next Five Years—Section 5B

Three figures are required to compute the average five-year return:

1. Average annual earnings per share over next five years.
2. Average percent of payout.
3. Present price.

The average earnings per share can be found on the EPS projection line on any SSG you complete. Simply look as the SSG Visual Analysis graph on Page 1 and read where the EPS projection line crosses the middle (3rd) year of the five projected years. The right margin is the 5th year.

Next, multiply this average EPS by the average payout ratio (found in Section 3, box 7G), to estimate the average annual dividend per share. When the average dividend per share is divided by the present price of the common stock, you have the estimated average annual yield over the next five years.

Average Yield–Johnson & Johnson

Average EPS for the next
five years   = $ 3.25
Average % payout   =   36.3%
Present stock price
per share   = $54.79
3.25 x 36.3   =   118.0
118.0 / 54.79   =   2.2%

Estimated Annual Total Return over Next Five Years—Section 5C

The estimated total annual return over the next five years is the average annual price gain plus the average annual yield. This is computed as follows:

Step 1. Divide the five-year percent of price appreciation (4E) by 5.

Step 2. If a dividend is paid, add the average yield (5B).

2 EVALUATING MANAGEMENT

Company **JOHNSON & JOHNSON**   (JNJ)   01/17/03

		1993	1994	1995	1996	1997	1998	1999	2000	2001	2002	LAST 5 YEAR AVG.	TREND UP	TREND DOWN
A	% Pre–tax Profit on Sales (Net Before Taxes ÷ Sales)	16.5	17.0	17.6	18.7	20.2	21.3	21.1	22.7	24.8	26.4	23.3	UP	
B	% Earned on Equity (E/S ÷ Book Value)	31.3	27.8	26.1	26.1	26.2	26.4	25.5	25.3	24.0	27.8	25.8	UP	

3 PRICE–EARNINGS HISTORY as an indicator of the future

This shows how stock prices have fluctuated with earnings and dividends. It is a building block for translating earnings into future stock prices.

PRESENT PRICE **54.790**   HIGH THIS YEAR **65.890**   LOW THIS YEAR **41.400**

	Year	A PRICE HIGH	B PRICE LOW	C Earnings Per Share	D Price Earnings Ratio HIGH A ÷ C	E Price Earnings Ratio LOW B ÷ C	F Dividend Per Share	G % Payout F ÷ C X 100	H % High Yield F ÷ B X 100
1	1998	44.9	31.7	1.34	33.6	23.7	0.485	36.3	1.5
2	1999	53.4	38.5	1.49	36.0	25.9	0.545	36.7	1.4
3	2000	53.0	33.1	1.71	31.0	19.4	0.620	36.3	1.9
4	2001	61.0	40.3	1.91	31.9	21.1	0.700	36.6	1.7
5	2002	65.9	41.4	2.25	29.3	18.4	0.800	35.6	1.9
6	TOTAL		185.0		161.8	108.5		181.5	
7	AVERAGE		37.0		32.4	21.7		36.3	
8	AVERAGE PRICE EARNINGS RATIO	27.1							
9	CURRENT PRICE EARNINGS RATIO				24.7				

Proj. P/E [21.84] Based on Next 4 qtr. EPS [2.51]   Current P/E Based on Last 4 qtr. EPS [2.22]

4 EVALUATING RISK and REWARD over the next 5 years

Assuming one recession and one business boom every 5 years, calculations are made of how high and how low the stock might sell. The upside–downside ratio is the key t

A HIGH PRICE –– NEXT 5 YEARS
Avg. High P/E **32.4**   **25.0** (3D7 as adj.)   X Estimate High Earnings/Share **4.15**   = Forecast High Price $ **103.8** (4A1)

B LOW PRICE –– NEXT 5 YEARS
(a) Avg. Low P/E **21.7**   **18.0** (3E7 as adj.)   X Estimated Low Earnings/Share **2.25**   = $ **40.5**
(b) Avg. Low Price of Last 5 Years = **37.0** (3B7)
(c) Recent Severe Market Low Price = **40.3**
(d) Price Dividend Will Support   Present Divd. (H) = **0.840** / High Yield **0.019**   = **43.5**
Selected Estimate Low Price   = $ **40.5** (4B1)

C ZONING
103.8 (4A1) High Forecast Price Minus **40.5** (4B1) Low Forecast Price Equals **63.3** (C)   Range. 1/3 of Range = **21.1** (4CD)

(4C2) Lower 1/3 = (4B1) **40.5** to **61.6** (Buy)
(4C3) Middle 1/3 = **61.6** to **82.7** (Maybe)
(4C4) Upper 1/3 = **82.7** to **103.8** (4A1) (Sell)

Present Market Price of **54.790**   is in the   **Buy** (4C5)   Range

D UP–SIDE DOWN–SIDE RATIO (Potential Gain vs. Risk of Loss)
High Price (4A1) **103.8**   Minus Present Price **54.790**
Present Price **54.790**   Minus Low Price (4B1) **40.5**   = **49.0** / **14.3** = **3.4** To 1 (4D)

E PRICE TARGET (Note: This shows the potential market price appreciation over the next five years in simple interest terms.)
High Price (4A1) **103.8**
Present Market Price **54.790**   = (**1.895**) X 100 = (**189.5**) – 100 = **89.5** % Appreciation (4E)

Relative Value: 91.1%   Proj. Relative Value: 80.6%

5 5-YEAR POTENTIAL

This combines price appreciation with dividend yield to get an estimate of total return. It provides a standard for comparing incdme and

Note: Results are expressed as a simple rate; use the table below to convert to a compound rate.

A Present Full Year's Dividend $ **0.840**
Present Price of Stock $ **54.790**   = **0.015** X 100 = **1.5** (5A) Present Yield or % Returned on Purchase Price

B AVERAGE YIELD OVER NEXT 5 YEARS
Avg. Earnings Per Share Next 5 Years **3.25**   X Avg. % Payout (3G7) **36.3** = **118.0** = **2.2** % (5B)
Present Price $ **54.790**

C ESTIMATED AVERAGE ANNUAL RETURN OVER NEXT FIVE YEARS
5 Year Appreciation Potential (4E) **89.5** / 5 = **17.9** %
Average Yield (5B) = **2.2** %
Average Total Annual Return Over the Next 5 Years (5C) = **20.1** %

Table to Convert from Simple to Compound Rates

Simple Rate: 2 4 6 8 10 12 14 16 18 20 22 24 26 28 30 32 34 36 38 40 / 2 4 6 8 10 12 14 16 18 20 22 24

Figure 25-01: 5 Year Potential

Estimated Annual Total Return–Johnson & Johnson

Five-year % of price appreciation potential (from Section 4, box 4E)
= **89.5%**

Average yield over next five years (from Section 5, box 5B)
= **2.2%**

Annual appreciation potential
= **(89.5% / 5) = 17.9%**

Average total return
= **(17.9 + 2.2) = 20.1%**

This figure is the simple average annual total return, not the compounded rate of return. In the bottom right corner of Page 2 of the SSG, you will find a table to convert from the simple rate to a compound rate of growth.

Using the conversion table, we see that the 20.1% simple rate estimated above converts to a compound rate of approximately 15%.

What Does Section 5 Mean?

Remember that the SSG is best suited for growth-oriented stocks. This section is important because it shows how to calculate total return and what the dividend yield contributes. Your goal is a doubling of the value of your investment in five years. Some stocks may yield 2–3% in dividends and the appreciation may be 12–13%. That reaches our goal.

Common stocks that pay a dividend tend to have less volatility in their prices than stocks where the total return is derived entirely from price appreciation.

SUMMARY

The "Five-Year Potential" section of the SSG is a tool for estimating the arithmetic average total return from your selected stock within the next five years. Total return includes both price appreciation and dividends (yield).

KEY WORDS

DIVIDEND POLICY
DIVIDEND YIELD
AVERAGE EARNINGS PER SHARE
AVERAGE PAYOUT
ESTIMATED ANNUAL TOTAL RETURN
FIVE-YEAR POTENTIAL
SIMPLE RATE OF GROWTH
COMPOUND RATE OF GROWTH

QUESTIONS & ACTIVITIES

1. Explain what the dividend policy may tell you about the company's growth stage.

   ■

2. Calculate the yield on the present purchase price for the stock you are studying.

   ■

3. Locate the average earnings per share for the next five years for your stock.

   ■

4. Calculate your stock's average yield over the next five years.

   ■

5. Calculate your stock's average annual return over the next five years.

The Bottom Line

Chapter Goals–

After studying and reviewing this chapter, you will be able to:

- Answer the questions on Pages 3 and 4 of the SSG.
- Understand the relevance of each of the eight questions to your stock selection decision.

- Determine whether a stock qualifies as a growth stock.
- Determine whether a stock meets your investment needs.

Introduction

After completing Pages 1 and 2 of the SSG for the stock you are studying, you are ready for a final decision. On SSG Pages 3 and 4 (see the end of this chapter) you will answer a set of eight questions designed to help you reach a decision based on the data and calculations in the first two pages of the Stock Selection Guide and on several other important considerations.

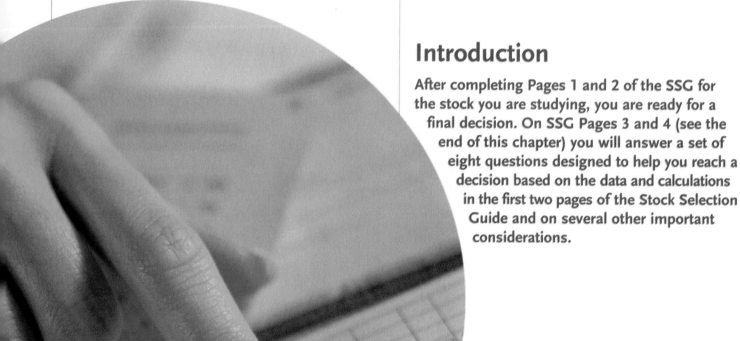

The Report Card and the Eight Questions–SSG Pages 3 and 4

At the top of SSG Page 3 is a "report card" on the stock you have just analyzed. You will grade the company (good, average, poor) in three main categories–judging management, evaluating price and weighing other considerations. And you will write your conclusion in the box provided.

The eight questions on SSG Pages 3 and 4 deal with the same areas you are asked to judge on your report card. They provide a concise review of the work you have done so far. You may find it more natural to respond to the eight questions first and then to complete the stock selection process by filling in the report card and writing your conclusion.

SSG Pages 3 and 4

Complete Pages 3 and 4 for the stock you are studying and then reach your own conclusion. Would you buy this stock now, based on your analysis?

The Rule of Five

It is good to keep in mind that the Stock Selection Guide (SSG) is just that, a guide with no guarantees attached to it. One of the founders of the NAIC—the man who developed the Stock Selection Guide—cautioned that, for every five stocks you select with the SSG, one is likely to have unexpected trouble, three will probably meet your expectations and one may well perform better you predicted. It is the average performance of the portfolio that will help you achieve your goal of doubling value every five years.

GOALS IN SELECTING A STOCK

You want to look ahead five years by **judging** Management capability and **evaluating** the Price you should pay for a stock. You should also look at **Other Considerations** and reach a **Conclusion. Your findings are registered in the table at the right and your Conclusion below.**

Novice and professional investors to varying degrees may act hastily on new products, tips, technical clues and short term factors rather than being methodical in their decisions. Thirty years of experience with this type of report tends to show that there is a RULE OF FIVE, which is this: If five companies are analyzed for their five year future, one may have unforeseeable trouble, three may be on target, and one may have unpredictable good fortune.

CONCLUSION: _____

_____

_____

_____

(1) Our goal is to find a company with **able** MANAGEMENT; and (2) to buy a stock at a **good** PRICE.

	Page	Good	Average	Poor
Judging Management				
Driving Force	3			
Earned on Sales	3			
Earned on Equity	3			
Evaluating Price				
High in 5 Years	4			
Low in 5 Years	4			
Upside-Downside Ratio	4			
Yield Current	4			
Total Return	4			
Other Considerations				
Industry Potentials	4			
State of Business Cycle	4			
Stock Price Trends	4			
Quality of Stock	4			
Capitalization and Finance	2			

METHOD-DATA-INSTRUCTIONS

This report organizes data presentation in a concise professional manner, avoiding among other things the agony of deciding what factors to cover. Because writing is a chore, the cross-out-method lets you report your judgments with ease. The data used comes from Value Line Reports that are available on many listed and unlisted companies. You may wish to check your 5 year "high estimate" with Value Line's estimated Target Price Range for 3 to 5 years hence. Instructions for

completing pages 3 and 4 of this report are in the *Investors Manual* obtainable from the National Association of Investors Corporation, P.O. Box 220, Royal Oak, Michigan 48068. Other sources of data are annual and quarterly reports from companies, brokers reports and visits to company annual meetings. You may learn by yourself, or with several friends, or by actually investing $20 or $50 a month through an investment club you have formed with friends.

1 WHAT DOES THE VISUAL ANALYSIS SHOW?

The trend of (sales) (revenues) is (up) (down) (sideways).

The trend of earnings per share is (up) (down) (sideways).

The price trend of the stock is (up) (down) (sideways).

If sales trend is up, the increase seems to have come from (taking a greater share of the market) (mergers and acquisitions) (new products or new product applications produced by research).

In my opinion, the stock should be (investigated) (discarded) because the trend of sales is (favorable) (neutral) (unfavorable); the trend of earnings per share is (favorable) (neutral) (unfavorable); the price is (favorable) (neutral) (unfavorable).

Also for other reasons as follows: _____

_____

_____

_____

_____

_____

2 DOES THE COMPANY PASS THE THREE MANAGEMENT TESTS?

Investors lose money because of failing to test for good management. Instead they rely on outlook for the industry, new products, or a plausible story for protection and often lose.

TEST I: DRIVING FORCE OF MANAGEMENT
Management as indicated by the past record has the necessary ability to expand sales (yes) (no). The rate of sales expansion on the VISUAL ANALYSIS looks like _____ % annually. The rate of sales expansion is likely to be (better) (same) (worse) in the next five years.

TEST II: EARNED ON SALES
Management seems to have the ability to (maintain) (increase) profit margins (see 2A, Evaluating Management on page 2 at left). It shows the Pre-Tax Profit Margins for each of the last five years as follows in

chronological order:

_____ %, _____ %, _____ %, _____ %, _____ %.

TEST III: EARNED ON EQUITY
The company has earned on invested capital from _____ % to _____ %. See 2B, Evaluating Management on page 2 at left. Earnings on equity are (above) (below) 10%.

I conclude from these three tests that the company has (good) (average) (poor) management and will be (stronger) (same) (weaker) in five years.

Over a period of five years, a well-managed company will generally gain ground while a poor one loses its earning power. Remember this in making your decision.

continued . . .

Figure 26-01: SSG Page 3

3 WHAT IS THE PRICE RANGE LIKELY TO BE FOR THE NEXT FIVE YEARS?

Complete Section 3 of the Stock Selection Guide & Report (page 2). Two considerations are important: (1) It is usually better to project sales and apply profit margins and taxes than to project earnings per share on the chart because profit margins tend to have definite upside limits; and (2) it is well to pay less attention to, or discard the much higher price-earnings ratios existing in years of low earnings. Also, avoid being misled by sales increases in early years of a new product or attributable to government or other types of contracts that may not be renewed or are due entirely to the upswing of a business cycle.

Have price-earnings (P/E) ratios for the past five years been trending (downward) (level) (upward)? Is the P/E ratio (higher) (same) (lower) than its competitors? Have the average price earnings ratios of the

past five years been influenced by years when the ratio was (unusually high) (unusually low)?

Over the next five years, the stock might be expected to reach a high price of _____ and also a low of _____ when the next depression comes. It now sells at _____ , indicating (little) (average) (great) risk. Its suggested buy prices should range from _____ to _____ , hold from _____ to _____ , and sell from _____ to _____ .

These are the zones calculated in the Stock Selection Guide & Report (Section 4C, page 2). Be a careful buyer.

4 HOW DOES THE STOCK MEET THE THREE SAFETY TESTS OF PRICE?

Unsuccessful investment clubs and investors make two mistakes: (1) selection of poorly managed companies. (2) pay too much for stocks. The second mistake is by far the most prevalent and most damaging, and is easily corrected. Big losses have been taken in high grade stocks because they were bought mainly, "because they were moving" or sold "because they went down" —not because of price. The best results have been obtained by investors that buy carefully.

TEST I: SHOWS PROBABILITY OF GETTING OUT EVEN
The stock under review has sold at its present price in (_____)* (none) of the last five years. The risk of loss seems (small) (average) (considerable) at the present price on the basis of price history.

* *Three of five is a good standard.*

TEST II: STACK THE ODDS IN THE INVESTORS FAVOR
The upside-downside ratio from Section 4D, page 2 of the Stock Selection Guide & Report is _____ to 1. This is (favorable) (average) (unfavorable), indicating that we need to pay attention to past price history (considerably) (some) (not much).

TEST III: THESE STANDARDS HELP INVESTORS AVOID LOSS
The pay-off test is whether at least 100% appreciation is possible in five years—or in the case of cyclical stocks, 20% a year for the number of years held. Analysis shows a high price of _____ is reasonable in _____ years, equal to _____ % a year.

In the case of cyclical stocks, comment should include the number of months the cycle has advanced and the dangers on this account.

5 WHAT ARE THE INVESTMENT CHARACTERISTICS OF THE COMPANY?

The Company is (well established) (new) and operates (internationally) (nationally) (regionally). The product line or service is (diversified) (narrow) and sold to (consumers) (manufacturers) (government). The business cycle affects sales and earnings (not much) (severely) (average). The company is (largest) (in top four) (a smaller factor) in its industry. The company and products are (well known) (average)

(not known) to the investing public. Its common stock is listed on (New York) (American) (other exchange) (unlisted) and has price records covering (five years) (only _____ years. It has (a continuous dividend record dating from _____) (a spotty dividend record) (no dividend record). Investment characteristics are (good) (average) (poor).

6 WHAT ARE THE CHARACTERISTICS OF THE COMPANY'S MAJOR INDUSTRY?

The _____ industry is (established) (new) and has (exceptional) (average) (below average) potential. The potential is based on (population) (product development) (science) (international expansion). Sales, profit margins and earnings per share fluctuate with the business cycle (widely—like the steel industry) (narrowly—like food) (average—like oil). Capital investment per dollar of sales in the industry is (high—like chemicals) (low—like clothing manufacture) (aver-

age—like metal products manufacturing), making it (easy) (difficult) for new competition to enter the business. Price competition between companies is (no problem) (severe) (average).

In my opinion, the major industry, everything considered, is (favorable) (average) (unfavorable). The company being analyzed will be (aided by the trend of the industry) or (will have to take business from competitors to grow).

7 WHAT ABOUT THE BUSINESS CYCLE?

About 33 months is an average business cycle, though variations from this norm are wide.

A well-managed company gains on marginal competitors in a depression or inflation as a general rule. In a period of business recovery, high grade stocks advance first, second grade stocks next, and marginal stocks last, as a general rule. Also, non-growth cyclical stocks are good purchases when business

turns up and should be sold in the later stages of the cycle because of exposure to substantial drops in price, earnings, and sometimes dividends.

The trend of business has been (up) (down) for _____ months. The current stage of the business cycle tends to (help) (not affect) (hurt) profits of the company. The present stage of the business cycle suggests (no concern) (caution) (daring) for the stock under review.

8 WHAT ABOUT THE STOCK MARKET AND YIELDS ON BONDS?

The price the stock is selling at is _____ and the Dow Jones Averages are at: Industrials _____ , Transportation _____ and Utilities _____ . *This provides a reference in case of review of this stock in the future.*

From the Value Line, it is seen that the stock under review has performed, as compared relatively (better) (same) (below).

You may also want to comment on the behavior of bond yields and Treasury Bill rates. Yields tend to rise in the later stages of a business cycle (attracting money from the stock market) and fall when business slows and investors want safety.

Bond yields may (attract) (not affect) (discourage) investment in this stock currently

Figure 26-02: SSG Page 4

Computer Programs

NAIC has a library of excellent software programs. Once you have mastered the printed Stock Selection Guide and have an understanding of what the figures tell you and how much you must rely on your own judgment, you may want to begin using one of the NAIC stock evaluation software programs in order to save time. *NAIC's Investor's Toolkit* software and *NAIC Classic* software provide computerized capabilities in completing a SSG and other NAIC stock selection forms. In addition, NAIC's "Online Premium Service" (OPS) provides Web site based company data for thousands of companies that are automatically entered into SSG's, using *Toolkit* or *Classic* software. Different member-ship categories offer a wealth of computerized investing information in the form of a regular electronic newsletter (*BITS Online*), workshops, and book and software discounts.

SUMMARY

The Stock Selection Guide can help you identify good, well-managed growth companies whose stocks are selling at reasonable prices today and have the potential to double in five years. The NAIC's goal is for you to start an investment program now while you are still young, and because of it, to achieve a better quality of life.

PROJECTS

1. How does filling in the Pages 3 and 4 of the SSG relate to the work you did on the first two pages?

    ■

2. The SSG is a tool for analyzing the fundamentals of a stock and a guide for estimating the appropriate buy price range of that stock. (True or False)

Appendix

STOCK SELECTION GUIDE CHECKLIST

The Stock Selection Guide is intended to help you select high-quality growth companies.

You should seek companies to study with ten years of historical operating data.

Do not rely on the guide to evaluate companies with less than five years of historical operating data.

1. **Fill in the upper right corner.**
   - Name of company being studied
   - The date of the study
   - Source of information
   - Where the stock is traded
   - Company's product or service
   - Number of preferred and common shares outstanding
   - Percent of debt to capitalization
   - Potential dilution

2. **Fill in the upper left.**
   - Last given quarterly figures for sales and earnings
   - Same quarter a year ago sales and earnings
   - Calculate the percentage of change

3. **Note when the fiscal year ends. This will help determine which ten years to use for your study.**

4. **Write the years to be used in the designated spaces at the bottom of the page.**

5. **Check the ranges of the sales and earnings to determine where they will fit in the cycles.**

6. **Plot the sales for the last ten years.**

7. **Plot the earnings per share for the last ten years.**

8. **Plot the common stock prices (high & low) for the last ten years.**

9. **Calculate and draw the trend lines for sales and earnings per share.**

10. **Complete section 2A by averaging the last five years and identifying the trend.**

11. **Complete section 2B by averaging the last five years and identifying the trend.**

12. **Calculate and draw the projection lines for sales and earnings per share.**

13. **Note the sales and earnings projections for the future five years in the right hand margin.**

14. **Find the present price, the high price of the last 52 weeks, the low price of the last 52 weeks and enter in the proper spaces at the top of section 3.**

15. **Complete section 3 as explained on the guide.**

16. **Complete section 4 as explained on the guide.**

17. **Complete section 5 as explained on the guide.**

18. **Answer the eight questions on SSG pages 3 and 4.**

19. **Fill in the goals section at the top of SSG page 3.**

20. **Write your conclusion.**

APPENDIX

APPENDIX 2

A GUIDE TO SELECTING GROWTH STOCKS

1. Complete all parts of the Stock Selection Guide.

2. Small to medium size companies should have a history of 15% growth or better in sales and earnings. Large companies may have growth of 7% to 10%, or better.

3. Sales and earnings should be advancing at approximately the same rate.

4. The most recent quarterly sales and earnings growth should be as high as the historical growth rate.

5. Price bars should be progressing upward showing that the price has doubled in the last five years.

6. Pre-tax profits should be growing at rates similar to sales and EPS.

7. Large growth companies represent buying opportunities on price dips while earnings are moving upward. This opportunity may come when the market is down, but the company's fundamentals remain strong.

8. The pre-tax profit on sales should be at a superior level and/or trending upward.

9. Percent earned on equity should be at a superior level and/or trending upward.

10. It is desirable for the growth rate of EPS to be equal to or less than the P/E.

11. The current P/E ratio, section 3 line 9, should be at or near the mid-point P/E, section 3 line 8.

12. The current price should be in the buy zone, preferably with a 3 to 1 or better upside/downside ratio.

13. The estimated five-year price appreciation should be 100% or better.

14. The total annual return (dividends and appreciation) should be a non-compounded 20% or better.

RULES FOR THE SUCCESSFUL INVESTOR

1. Be patient.
- The stock market goes up and down.
- The best buys are made when the company's fundamentals are good, but the stock market is down.

2. Don't be a chronic stock switcher.
- Commissions are costly on small stock purchases.
- Small investors should use low-cost means of investing: NAIC's Low Cost Investment Plan, DRIPS, direct purchases from companies, participation in an investment club.

3. Don't be overly concerned with price changes.
- Popularity produces over-popularity.
- By study and comparison, choose stocks before everybody is climbing on the bandwagon.

4. Invest in vigorous growth companies.
- They are the most profitable.
- They are the easiest to analyze.

5. Look for real sleepers.
- Study pays off in greater gains for you.
- Find these companies before the institutional investors find them.

6. Make sure the price is reasonable.
- Buy only in the buy zone.
- Stay near or below the average 5-year mid-point P/E ratio.

7. Do not over-reach for yields.
- Favor companies that retain much of their earnings.
- Growth companies need to invest earnings in future growth.
- Be careful when companies pay out a large percentage of their earnings as dividends.

8. Be wary of low-priced stock promotions.
- Price is no indication of value.
- What you want is value and growth potential.

9. Be slow to average down (dollar cost average when the price is falling).
- If you have a loss, give the stock time to calm down and stabilize before adding to it.
- It is best to average up by adding to stocks in a rising pattern.

10. Do not insist on owning the most active stocks.
- Better values often exist in less popular stock.
- It pays to shop around.
- Use NAIC's stock analysis tools.

11. Review your stocks periodically.
- Use the NAIC's Portfolio Management Guide.
- If you make a mistake, face it frankly and move on.
- Try to learn something from stocks that do not perform as you expected.

12. Diversify, but not too widely.
- Diversity means different companies, different size companies, and different industries.
- But don't create a portfolio that is too diverse to watch and manage.

BUY GROWTH STOCKS. HOLD FOR THE LONG TERM.

●

THAT IS THE WAY WEALTH IS ACCUMULATED.

●

THAT IS THE WAY MILLIONAIRES ARE MADE!

Index

INDEX

Pass on the Gift of Lifetime Investing!

Send a Free NAIC Investor's Kit to a Family Member or Friend

Help a family member, friend, neighbor or co-worker become a successful long-term investor... the NAIC Way! Send us their name and we will mail them a free NAIC Investor's Kit. This kit will include information introducing them to NAIC long-term investment methods, programs and tools. The kit will also explain the benefits of lifetime investing including guidelines for starting an investment program on your own or with an investment club.

To send a free NAIC Investor's Kit to someone you know - complete the information below and mail, fax or e-mail the information to NAIC, or contact NAIC by calling toll free: 1-877-275-6242.

Help others you know become successful long-term investors... *the NAIC way!*

Mail to:
NAIC
P.O. Box 220
Royal Oak, MI 48068

____ **YES, please send an NAIC Investor's Kit
to the following person:**

Name _____

Address_____

City_____State_____Zip_____

e-mail _____

FAX: 248-583-4880
e-mail: service@better-investing.org
NAIC Web Site: www.better-investing.org

185

NAIC®

Investment Education Since 1951

The National Association of Investors Corporation (NAIC) is a non-profit organization of individual investors and investment clubs, based in Madison Heights, Michigan. Founded in 1951, NAIC's mission is to increase the number of individual investors through investing in common stocks and equity mutual funds, and to provide a program of investment education and information to help its members become successful, long-term investors. NAIC helps investors start a lifetime investment program by following NAIC's Four Investment Principles:

1) *Invest a set sum regularly over your lifetime*
2) *Reinvest earnings and dividends*
3) *Buy growth stocks and mutual funds that concentrate on growth companies.*
4) *Diversify your investments*

NAIC members who follow these investment principles have become successful investors over time.

To learn how to start a lifetime investment program using NAIC's proven methods, contact NAIC today.

National Association of Investors Corporation
711 West 13 Mile Road
Madison Heights, MI 48071
1-877-ASK-NAIC (275-6242)
www.better-investing.org